A Man's Man Called by God

Paul J. Jorden, M.D.
with Carole Sanderson Streeter

While this book is designed for the reader's personal enjoyment
and profit, it is also intended for group study. A Leader's Guide
with Victor Multiuse Transparency Masters is available from your
local bookstore or from the publisher at $2.95.

VICTOR BOOKS
a division of SP Publications, Inc.
WHEATON, ILLINOIS 60187

Offices also in Fullerton, California • Whitby, Ontario, Canada • Amersham-on-the-Hill, Bucks, England

Cover art by Joe Van Severen

Unless otherwise noted, Scripture quotations are from the *New American Standard Bible* (NASB), © 1960, 1962, 1968, 1971, 1972, 1973 by The Lockman Foundation, La Habra, California. Other quotations are from the King James Version (KJV); the *New International Version* (NIV), © 1978 by the New York International Bible Society; *The New Berkeley Version in Modern English* (BERK), © 1945, 1959, 1969 by the Zondervan Publishing House. Used by permission.

Recommended Dewey Decimal Classification: 220.92
Suggested Subject Headings: OLD TESTAMENT—BIOGRAPHY, DAVID;
1 AND 2 SAMUEL

Library of Congress Catalog Card Number: 80-50675
ISBN: 0-88207-220-X

VICTOR BOOKS
A division of SP Publications, Inc.
P.O. Box 1825 • Wheaton, Illinois 60187

To the Homebuilders Class

whose vigorous discussion added so much

to my understanding of David

To Sue

my daughter and personal secretary

who is 18 going on 25

SCALE OF MILES

0   10   20   30   40

SYRIAN TERRITORY

Tyre

PHOENICIA

GESHURITES

BASHAN

SEA OF CHINNERETH

THE GREAT SEA
(MEDITERRANEAN)

Mt. Tabor

En-dor

Shunem

Jezreel

Beth-shan

Jabesh-gilead

Mahanaim

CANAANITES

Mt. Gilboa

Aphek

Shiloh

Mt. Ephraim

Ophrah

Bethel

Beth-horon

Michmash

Ekron

Mizpeh

Ramah

Rabbah

Beth-shemesh

Gibeon

Gibeah

Jericho

AMMON

Ashdod

Kirjath-jearim

Nob

Gilgal

Ashkelon

Jerusalem

PHILISTIA

Bethlehem

Gath

Adullam

DEAD SEA

Keilah

Tekoa

Hebron

Ziph

En-gedi

Ziklag

Carmel

Maon

Beer-sheba

JUDAH

MOAB

Hormah

KENITES

ISRAEL
UNDER SAUL
AND DAVID

AMALEKITES

AMORITES

EDOM

CONTENTS

FOREWORD

Physicians have a hard time living in a world of wishes. Reality keeps getting their attention. People come to them with broken limbs and shattered health, and in the process expose their broken hearts, shattered dreams, and ruined homes. Physicians see people, warts and all. Perhaps that's why Paul Jorden, a physician, has been fascinated with David.

More space in the Bible is devoted to David than to any other man—more even than to the life of Jesus. Four Old Testament books feature his life story. David's own writings, many of them candidly revealing, fill at least 73 chapters.

The Bible does not offer us its heroes wrapped in cellophane but with the dirt of life upon them. For example, ask the man in the street what he knows about David, and he will probably answer in terms of David's greatest victory or his worst defeat. As a boy David killed Goliath, and as a man he committed adultery with Bathsheba and murdered her husband, Uriah.

Many parents who named their sons *David* might have entertained second thoughts if they had read his biography. For mothers who feel that good boys ought not fight, and for Christians who believe that good men do not sin (at least very badly), David can be hard to handle. Yet, of all the men who have ever lived, David is singled out as "a man after God's own heart."

A doctor who takes life histories, and meets people at their worst and their best, will not be shocked by David. Perhaps better than other men, the doctor will understand and appreciate him. That proves to be the case in Dr. Paul Jorden's discussion of this improbable saint.

Haddon Robinson, President
Conservative Baptist Theological Seminary
Denver, Colorado

7

INTRODUCTION

A man's man like David is not often found in the church. He would intimidate too many people. David was a rugged man who could survive alone in the rough terrain of Judah. He was strong enough to kill a lion, and brave enough to confront and fell Goliath. He was winsome enough to enjoy the love of many women.

David's personality was complex, and he gave himself intensely to whatever he was doing. His emotional valleys were extremely low and his peaks extremely high.

He was a leader of men, able to win and retain loyalties over long periods of time, from a position of weakness as well as strength.

Both versatile and adaptable, David was a man of extreme contrasts. He was a shepherd, a fugitive, a king, as well as the poet who composed psalms so poignant that they have inspired people for centuries. He was the skilled and sensitive musician who calmed the evil temperament of Saul. David could vigorously lead his people in worship, yet order the murder of one of his friends. He refused to see his own son for five years, then wept inconsolably at Absalom's death.

David was called a man after God's heart because God had confidence in him. David obeyed God as sovereign Lord, and considered himself God's servant. "I have found David the son of Jesse, a man after My heart, who will do all My will" (Acts 13:22).

I hope that you will find David's God in a new way as you take another look at this most unusual man. David was a man's man called by God from the ordinary life of a shepherd to the extraordinary life of king of Israel. Though his colorful personality qualifies David as "the most unforgettable character I will ever meet," I must not forget that his confidence was not in himself but in God.

Sooner or later even a man's man must recognize and come to grips with his Creator, his God. No man controls his own destiny. This truth comes through loud and clear in David's life.

Paul J. Jorden, M.D.

8

1
From the Ordinary into the Extraordinary

1 SAMUEL 16—17

The scene must have been one of significant contrast as the elderly and esteemed Prophet Samuel looked at the handsome and muscular young man before him. The anointing oil ran down from David's ruddy hair onto his shepherd cloak and to the ground, marking the spot where he was anointed as the future king of Israel.

Samuel had carried the bottle of oil from his house, as he walked from Ramah early that morning. He had been sent by God to the home of Jesse in Bethlehem, to anoint one of Jesse's sons. For God had rejected Saul as king.

As the seven older sons had appeared before him, Samuel had

been sure that Eliab was the one. But God had made it clear that none of the seven was the future king.

Then Samuel had asked, "Are these all your sons?"

Jesse had replied, "Oh, the youngest one is out with the sheep." No one had thought to call David for an impromptu religious ceremony. He was just a teenager.

But God wanted him there; for God frequently chooses teenagers, and children too as His friends, and prepares them to move from the ordinary into the extraordinary.

The Sign of Belonging

As David was anointed in the quiet family ceremony, the Spirit came upon him, from that day on (16:13). We are not told whether David or his family knew the full significance of the anointing at that time. He didn't know exactly where that anointing would take him, any more than we know where our walk with God will take us. But David must have felt a distinct difference in his life after that day, as the Spirit of God made known His presence and did His work of preparation in David.

When we come into a family relationship with God, we too are anointed by the Holy Spirit who resides within us as a seal from God. We have this family relationship with God through the Person of His Son, Jesus Christ, who makes it possible for us to call God our Father. Therefore, it is our privilege, as it was David's, to follow the leading of the Lord into His plan for our lives.

As an infant, I had diphtheria and was not expected to live. My grandfather, who was a minister, stayed in my room an entire night, praying that God would spare my life. During the long night, my Christian mother dedicated me to the service of God. Obviously, at that time I was not aware of their prayers for me.

However, I do recall kneeling in my bedroom all alone when I was 12 years old, and receiving Jesus Christ as my personal Saviour. Although I had been a good boy in home and school, I still recognized that I was a sinner. From that moment on, I knew that there was a different relationship between me and God. That sense of relationship with God has lasted to this day.

I must confess at times I actually admire people who have spectacular testimonies—people who have been robbers, drunkards, or prostitutes, who have met the Lord in a startling manner. But this was not my story, nor was it David's.

Struggling Saul

The people of Israel had wanted a king and God had chosen Saul to be that king. Saul was struggling during his reign because he was repeatedly disobedient to God. He had been dealt with many times by God, giving him opportunity to repent. However, he would not do so, and finally the Spirit of the Lord departed from Saul and "an evil spirit from the Lord terrorized him" (16:14).

This evil spirit was the very cause that would bring David into the court of Saul, so that these two chosen men of God could become acquainted with one another. David needed to go to court to learn about being the king. The servants of Saul suggested that a man be found who could skillfully play the harp, so the music would soothe the evil spirit which troubled Saul. When Saul agreed to this, one of his servants just happened to know about a son of Jesse. He was an accomplished musician, a brave soldier, a fine speaker, good-looking, and a godly person. Wow! What a reputation! What a man!

I don't believe we can consider it a coincidence that the servant knew of David. In the life of a child of God, there are no accidents. God is always controlling circumstances to accomplish His purposes. In an unusual way He brought His two men together.

Saul asked Jesse to send David to him; and Jesse, following the culture of the time, sent bread and wine as well as a sheep with David. Immediately, Saul loved the youth and made him his armor bearer. He sent word to Jesse saying, "Let David now stand before me; for he has found favor in my sight" (16:22). What a compelling presence and personality David must have had!

When the evil spirit came upon Saul, David took his harp and played so beautifully that Saul was refreshed, and the evil spirit departed from him. I believe that David played sacred music;

and this challenges me as a father of nine children to keep a good choice of music available in my home, as well as in my car. I struggle with popular music and its volume as played by teenagers. I think we need to realize the power of sacred music to settle ruffled nerves and bad spirits. Even though our children may object vigorously to our choice, we must keep it available to them as an option. I think sacred music in the house is more important than wall-to-wall carpeting!

Leaders Are Followers First

When Saul was calm again, God sent David back to be subject to his father. You see, God cannot use a leader who is not first a follower. God was preparing David to be a king, and so He sent him back for another course in being a shepherd—alone with God, alone with the sheep. Thus God could teach him, mold him, and make him into the man who would be capable of leading Israel.

As parents, we must teach our children to obey. If one of our children has the potential of being a leader, we must teach him to be a follower first. This is done by teaching him to obey. Despite his success before King Saul, David was still subject to his father Jesse. Despite the fact that Jesus Himself, at 12 years of age, stayed behind in the temple to converse with the elders, He still returned to His parents' home and was subject to them.

Over and over in the Word of God, we are instructed to teach our children to obey. It doesn't matter how successful they are or what their potential is. Our job as parents is to teach them to obey. Jesse had done this well. He now told his youngest son, "Take these things and go and greet your brothers at the battlefront."

With some grain and bread for the brothers and 10 cuts of cheese for their commander—and after he had gotten someone to take care of his sheep—David left for the battleground. When he arrived at the Valley of Elah, he left his supplies with the baggage keeper.

Do you see David's sense of responsibility in small things? Even though he was a musician and shepherd, even though he was a man of bravery, he was careful about small details like sheep and baggage.

If you want your children to grow up to be responsible people, give them little things to be in charge of while they are young, and see that they carry them through. There is no way you can hand a teenager the keys to your car and expect responsibility if you have not taught responsibility in smaller matters years before.

Brotherly Love

After David got rid of his baggage, he ran down to find his brothers. As they were talking together, who should appear but Goliath—all 9½ feet of him. His vest alone weighed 16 pounds. Plus that, he wore a bronze helmet, bronze shin guards, and a bronze javelin slung between his shoulders. His spear weighed more than 15 pounds.

Goliath roared forth the challenge that had been terrifying Israel's army for 40 days: "Choose one man and let him come here. If he is able to fight with me and kill me, then we will become your servants. But if I kill him, then you will become our servants" (17:8-9).

Saul's army was scared. They talked about the "other guy," the one brave enough to take up Goliath's challenge and fight with him. David saw how frightened the army was of Goliath's words. He heard that the man who killed Goliath would be given great riches by King Saul, including one of Saul's daughters as his wife, thus making his household tax-free.

David's reaction to Goliath was significant. He was not looking on the giant as a man who challenged the army of Israel, but as a nonbeliever, an uncircumcised Philistine who was defying the living God. This made David's blood boil. He began asking questions of those standing nearby.

When his older brother Eliab heard what David was saying, his anger rose as he asked, "Why have you come down? Whom did you leave those few sheep with in the wilderness? I know how insolent and bad you are. You've just come down to see the battle!" (17:28)

David replied, "What have I done now? I just asked a question."

This sounds like something right out of my house. Recently, one of my teenage girls came to me just before I was to teach my Sunday School class. She wanted me to hear the true story before her brother found me. She had had a tussle with him at home, and in the process had torn the skin of her hand on his buckle and also had gotten quite a few bruises.

No matter how you try to raise your kids, there will always be sibling rivalry and conflict. Don't think you can have a house full of kids without this turmoil. David was the youngest of eight brothers, and he was experiencing the wrath of a brother coming down on him. Possibly some of this might have been justified. As a potential leader, David may have had great pride in himself and in his accomplishments.

Future Leaders

For a year our family of 11 lived and worked at a mission station in Africa. A couple of the missionary boys got into considerable trouble and the leaders of the mission came together to discuss how to handle this problem. One man made a significant statement: "Gentlemen, we must be very fair with these two boys. They come from a long, long line of missionary families, and you know that they might well end up as our field directors some day." All of us laughed because we knew he was right. Leaders sometimes have stormy pasts.

Kids who cause the most trouble are often the very ones who have gifts to be leaders. We can interpret their behavior as wildness, but they are more like mustangs. We parents have to guide them in the right direction, to saddle-break them without breaking their spirits. God has made them high-spirited for His glory. Our job is to appreciate their enthusiasm and direct them in the way God wants them to go. We shouldn't try to change them. To say, "Why can't you be docile and easy like your brother?" goes over like a big lead balloon!

Prepared for Battle

David didn't argue with his brother but kept on asking questions about Goliath until Saul heard about David and sent for him. He approached the king with amazing confidence: "Don't you worry about Goliath. I'll go fight with him."

Saul warned David that the giant was an experienced man of war. David countered by relating to Saul that while he was keeping his father's sheep, a lion and a bear had attacked the flock and he had killed both of them. Then David said, "This uncircumcised Philistine will be like one of them, since he has taunted the armies of the living God. God who delivered me from the paw of the lion and the bear will deliver me from the hand of this Philistine" (17:32-37).

David had confidence in himself, but his confidence was more than that. He knew his strength would be from God as he confronted the giant. Saul said to David, "Go and the Lord be with you." It seemed as if David's witness of confidence in God was reaching into Saul's heart. I believe, in Saul's awareness of God's presence, he was being given another opportunity to repent of his evil ways.

Saul then tried to put his armor on David. He wanted to give the boy some tools to do the job. But David had never worn armor before. He was simply a shepherd boy, and was wise enough not to use unfamiliar tools. God did not ask David to do something for which he was not prepared. He doesn't ask that of us either.

David dressed in all Saul's armor reminds me of my football games with my teenage sons and their friends. It is one thing to play touch football in your front yard without any football gear, and quite another to wear all the paraphernalia. If you put a helmet with face mask, and shoulder pads on a young man, it will take him considerable time to see the ball, much less catch it. You don't take a person from the sidelines, put him in full gear, and expect him to run a long pass pattern. He probably will fall flat on his face.

During our year in Africa there were many times I flew in single-engine planes with Missionary Aviation Fellowship pilots. On each flight I thought, *If something happens to this pilot, I am up a creek. I have never flown a plane.* I must admit that I watched the pilots every time we took off and landed to become more familiar with the instruments.

The point is you don't get into a plane and say, "In the power of God I am going to fly this thing." God doesn't work that way. He doesn't ask you to do what you are not prepared to do. I don't want anyone coming into my operating room and saying, "Paul, God tells me I ought to do this operation for you."

I would ask, "Have you been trained in surgery?"

"No, I've never been in an operating room before in my life, but God has called me to do this operation." Nobody should think that way. God certainly does not.

While David stood there nearly hidden by all Saul's armor, he thought, *I'm fighting for the living God. I don't need to use these things; I don't even know how to use them.* David got out of the armor, left the king, and walked down to the brook where he selected five smooth stones. Why smooth stones? Rough stones would follow an irregular course, when thrown from a sling. The smooth stones would be true to their mark.

Meeting the Enemy

As David walked toward Goliath, the giant and his armor bearer got a good look at this young and handsome man. Goliath sneered at David, "Am I a dog, that you come to me with sticks?" Then he cursed David by his gods, and said, "Come to me, and I will give your flesh to the birds of the sky and the beasts of the field."

Goliath had sneered at David's weapon, cursed him by heathen gods, and tried to intimidate him with a threat of death. David answered each part of Goliath's remarks.

You come to me with a sword, a spear, and a javelin, but I come to you in the name of the Lord of hosts, the God of the armies of Israel, whom you have taunted. This day the Lord will deliver you up into my hands, and I will strike you down and remove your head from you. And I will give the dead bodies of the army of the Philistines this day to the birds of the sky and the wild beasts of the earth, that all the earth may know that there is a God in Israel, and that all this assembly may know that the Lord does not deliver by sword or by spear; for the battle is the Lord's and He will give you into our hands (17:45-47).

A magnificent witness to a man about to die! Yes, David was a man after God's own heart—a man confident that God would prevail.

You might think David was being very foolish to approach Goliath with nothing but a sling and five smooth stones. But remember, he realized his own skill with that sling. In my own surgical practice, I have confidence in my training as well as in my skill as a surgeon. But I still feel the need to take a moment for quiet and personal prayer before any operation, to recognize that my success is in the hands of God. All I can do is put bones together. It is God who really heals!

As Goliath came nearer to meet David, the boy ran toward the giant. Taking a stone from his bag, he slung it and hit the Philistine with such force that the stone sank into Goliath's forehead, and he fell to the ground. Then David ran over to where Goliath lay and took the giant's own sword to cut off his head.

A person of Goliath's size would have a large forehead, making it an easy target. However, the forehead would also have been thick. David had to hit him with terrific force to knock Goliath unconscious and embed the stone into the bone. The Bible does not state that the stone killed Goliath, and chances are that it did not. However, decapitating the giant was a rather spectacular way to confirm his death.

When the Philistines saw what had happened, they fled; and the armies of Israel and Judah pursued them as far as the entrance to the valley, and to the gates of Ekron. When the Israelites returned from chasing and killing the Philistines, they plundered their empty camps. It is interesting how brave men can become, once the victory has been won!

David Who?

As David had gone out to fight with Goliath, King Saul had said to Abner, his general, "Who is this boy? Who is his father?" Abner didn't know, so when David returned from killing Goliath and carrying his head, Abner brought him before Saul.

Saul's lack of recognition of David has caused some Bible scholars to believe that this was a sign of the king's mental illness.

It does seem incredible that Saul would not remember David who had played the harp so beautifully that it had driven away the evil spirit which had plagued him.

We aren't sure about Saul's mental state, but I am more interested in David's reaction to the lack of recognition. He didn't seem disturbed. He hadn't entered the battle to be praised.

I have a good friend who used to spend much of his time traveling about the country, representing the Christian organization of which he was president. His impression was that 90 percent of the membership didn't even know who the president of the organization was. This is a little hard on the ego, but is often true to human experience.

Well on His Way

Already we see how God had prepared David to be king of Israel, to move from the pasture into the palace. First David ministered in music; then he witnessed to Saul of his confidence in God, and then gained a tremendous military victory with the most simplistic tools. The victory over Goliath would have given David further confidence in the meaning of his anointing, as well as bringing him to the attention of the nation.

The years David had spent with the sheep before this dramatic episode must have seemed rather dull and routine. Yet they included plenty of time to develop his gift in music and poetry, to relate to God's creation, and to become a rugged and physically skillful young man.

During his early years, David had developed confidence in himself and in his God, which now made him able to meet an extremely stressful situation with calm deliberation and decisiveness. He was also totally unembarrassed about expressing his faith in God to Saul, to Goliath, and to the soldiers of both armies. This is one mark of a person who has spent time with God.

In our very vigorous society, we often become so busy that we yearn for more solitude, more quiet time to spend with God. This is all well and good, but I really wonder—if we had more time, would we spend it with God? Or would we spend it in front of the television set, or behind the sports pages?

Active people are not going to be given long periods of solitude. Within our busy schedules, we have to make time to recognize God, to worship, to study, and then to witness to others of our confidence in God.

Each one of us has been called from the ordinary to the extraordinary adventure of being God's child and walking with Him. As David's life included what God had planned for him, so your life and mine can include those extraordinary plans that God has for us. And such a life calls for godly discipline along with consistent worship.

מָגֵן דָּוִד

2
Stepping Aside—
Ungraciously

1 SAMUEL 18—20

When I established my medical practice in Wheaton in 1963, I was the only orthopedic surgeon in a 10-mile radius. For several years, all of my patients were referred to me by other physicians, and they frequently waited four to six weeks for a routine appointment.

Although I was working very hard, I found my practice very satisfying, because I knew I was meeting a real need in my community.

However, in the following years other orthopedic surgeons opened offices in the Wheaton area, and now there are 12 of us. Of course the city has grown, but not by 12 times, and I have sensed my need to step aside somewhat, and let younger men take up part of the orthopedic care for this community.

At times, stepping aside can be a strain on one's ego. I've worked hard for the people in my town, and I still find it strange that not everybody wants to come to me. In fact, my self-image is such that I usually think that patients who have seen other orthopedists just weren't able to get an appointment with me!

In business firms this same type of situation is common. A man will have worked diligently for his company for many years, only to realize that a younger man is being hired to take over part or all of his responsibility. He may be told, "Move into a different position or resign." This threat to his livelihood and position within the company can cause all sorts of mental, physical, and emotional difficulties. The male ego suffers, and often the "male mid-life syndrome" makes its appearance. We have long recognized, and at times laughed at, the female menopause; but now it is becoming more and more clear that middle-aged men go through very significant changes in attitudes and capabilities.

Our study of David includes a situation of this type, only in proportions far more extreme than most men face today. Saul, as the first king of Israel, had a position of power and prestige unequaled in the nation. But through his disobedience, he had lost the favor of God, and knew he was going to be replaced. In the young hero David, he was confronted with his replacement.

Many people have felt that Saul was on the verge of insanity at this point in his life. I will admit that he did show symptoms of mental and emotional stress. But I believe that his difficulty was rooted in his personal arrogance, in years of disobedience to God, and that Saul was literally driving himself crazy, just as so many people are doing today.

The Young Hero David

David's triumph over Goliath had made him a national hero. It had also given him a confirming sign of his anointing as the future king, as well as confidence in his own personal powers.

But David's immediate problem was King Saul, and his reaction to David's military success and personal attractiveness. Saul was very ungracious as he saw this young and mighty man of valor coming into his life. It is easy for us to see that David was a threat to Saul and his position. But Saul's reactions certainly left something to be desired.

David and Jonathan

After David had finished his conversation with Saul and Abner, identifying himself as the son of Jesse, Saul's son Jonathan made it clear to his father that he would like David to stay. His soul "was knit to the soul of David, and Jonathan loved him as himself. And Saul took him that day and did not let him return to his father's house" (18:1-2).

Jonathan made a covenant of friendship with David, and as tokens of this, gave David his robe and armor, including his sword, bow, and belt.

Now it might seem strange that Jonathan was so enamored with David. But we have to remember that Jonathan was the young prince who had assaulted a garrison of Philistines with only one person to help him. (See 1 Sam. 14.) He had accomplished his brave deed in the name of the Lord, just as David had conquered Goliath.

When Jonathan saw David walking toward Saul and carrying Goliath's head under his arm, he saw a young man who had done an impossible thing in the strength of God. These young men were like two peas in a pod, and Jonathan must have thought, *Wow! This guy is just like a brother!*

In our day, we might blush at the idea of Jonathan loving David as his own soul. We will see that this love continued until Jonathan's death, and beyond; for later, David loved Jonathan's son. But we will also see that their relationship was honorable. There is no indication that they broke any of God's laws.

David and Saul

David was obedient to Saul. He had been well-trained by his father, and always went wherever Saul sent him, behaving himself wisely. Saul set David over the men of war, and David found acceptance among the people of the land, and also in the company of Saul's servants. Yes, Jesse had taught his youngest son well, to be obedient in the small things of life, so that now he could be faithful in larger responsibilities.

As Saul and his army traveled back to Gibeah after the slaughter of Goliath and the Philistines, women from all the cities they passed came running out to see the soldiers and the king. But they especially wanted to see David. They sang their songs: "Saul has slain his thousands, and David his ten thousands." This made Saul very angry and he said to himself, *They have ascribed to David ten thousands, but to me they have ascribed thousands. Now what more can he have but the kingdom?*

It is not difficult to relate to Saul and the deflation of his ego, along with the threat to his kingdom. Many of us have had young people come into our lives and into our businesses to threaten our positions.

If God brings into your life a young turk whom you think is still wet behind the ears, but who begins to show great promise in something that you do well, be very careful that you don't regard him with envy or malice. Instead, realize that God has allowed him to be part of your experience, and that He can teach you many things through this. God was trying to teach Saul to be obedient to His ways, but Saul never learned. He constantly saw David as a rival and threat, rather than as a means of grace.

Saul the Alienator

Some people seem to have a natural gift for alienating those close to them. Their actions frequently result from the way they relate to authority and to property.

Saul recognized no authority as being over him. He acted as if everything belonged to him—the kingdom, the office of prophet, the priests, the souls of his children.

Nothing restrained him, except his own fear. And in his more violent times, he did a good job of keeping his family in an uproar. For instance, he suddenly canceled his daughter's wedding. He threw swords at dinner guests. He planned to kill his son-in-law as well as his son. He asked his daughter to help him kill her husband. He humiliated his son in public.

Saul was under stress and did his best to put everyone around him under stress. And while all this seemed to stem from his fear of David, it really originated from his poor relationship to God and to the world around him.

If you ever feel as Saul did, don't think you must continue on the same downward road as he did. Finding the road back to obedience and humility may not be easy, and you may want to give up at times. But just as God was there to receive Saul—if he had repented and obeyed—so your heavenly Father waits for you to admit that you can't cope with all aspects of your life.

Promotion to Commander

From this point on, Saul looked on David with suspicion. Not long after they had returned home from the battlefront, Saul tried, not just once but twice, to pin David to the wall with his spear. Saul was afraid of David for two reasons: He knew the Lord had departed from him; and he knew the Lord was now with David.

I see patients who are javelin throwers. They leave work full of envy and hatred, get into their cars, throw them angrily into gear, and fly out of parking lots—right into pedestrians or other vehicles. Their javelins have four wheels! Many injuries and fatalities are the result of angry drivers. Such people are accidents going someplace to happen!

Saul now made an intelligent decision—he appointed David as commander over 1,000 men. This post would take him out of town. However, when David was back out with the people, he gained even more popularity, and prospered "in all his ways, for the Lord was with him" (18:14).

When someone is bugging you, it is wise to get him out of your presence. But unfortunately, out of sight is not always out of mind. And when Saul saw David's increased success, his fear became anguish.

Promotion to Son-in-law

Saul's next reaction to David was to offer Merab to him as his wife, if David would "be a valiant man . . . and fight the Lord's battles" (18:17). Then Saul could send David off to war, let the Philistines kill him, and be rid of him.

David's response was clearly humble—"Who am I, and what is my life or my father's family in Israel, that I should be the king's son-in-law?" Saul must have decided the same thing; by the time David got home from the battle, Merab was already married to someone else.

However, Saul's younger daughter Michal fell in love with David. When Saul's servants told him this, he was pleased, thinking he could accomplish the same thing through Michal as he had planned to through Merab. The deterioration of Saul's character was becoming more apparent, in his willingness to involve both of his daughters in a plot to see David dead.

Saul commanded his servants to speak to David secretly, saying that the king was delighted in David, that the king's servants loved him, and that he should marry Michal. When David objected, stating that he was a poor man and could not raise the bride price, the servants assured him that Saul desired nothing but 100 foreskins from the Philistines. The chance of David coming back from this alive seemed slight. Saul was ignoring one fact—David had already paid the bride price by killing Goliath.

Saul's challenge rang the bell of this mighty man, who promptly went out with his men and gathered not 100 but 200 foreskins to present to Saul. Typical of a man like David, he not only met the challenge, but doubled it!

After David and Michal were married, and Saul saw his daughter's love added to the favor of God in David's life, he was even more afraid of his new son-in-law. He now regarded himself as David's enemy. In subsequent battles with the Philistines, "David behaved himself more wisely than all the servants of Saul. So his name was highly esteemed" (18:30).

Father and Son
Saul now turned to Jonathan and to his servants, asking them to kill David. Saul had counted on the Philistines to do the job for him, but now they would have to do it themselves. Saul's decline in judgment is shown in asking Jonathan to help in this murder.

He knew of the special affection between the two young men. Jonathan's response was just what we might have expected—he warned David that his life was in danger and suggested that he hide in a safe place until Jonathan had a chance to talk with the king.

Jonathan's words to his father had heavy overtones as he stressed the sinfulness of Saul's wish, David's selfless bravery for the country, and the personal benefit which Saul had reaped from David's actions. He also spoke of David's innocence and the fact that his father had no cause for what he was planning. Saul saw the point and swore that as the Lord lived, David would not be killed. Then Jonathan called David to come back with the family.

It would be nice to say that the three lived happily ever after; and they might have, except that there was another war. When David gained a great victory, the evil spirit came back to Saul. Later, they were all sitting in the palace and David was playing the harp for Saul. Suddenly, Saul tried again to pin David to the wall, but David was fast on his feet and the spear penetrated deep into the wall.

What about David? Why did he run? He was the anointed of the Lord—shouldn't he just have stayed where he was and expected God to protect him? If you have someone in your life who is trying to harm you, it is foolish just to stand there and let him do whatever he wishes and expect God to protect you. God wants you to use wisdom and common sense.

Some risks I see believers taking make me nervous, because I think they are being very foolhardy. David was very much aware of the danger of being around Saul. When he saw the javelin in Saul's hand, and noticed that the king's arm was getting fidgety, he moved out of the way, fast. God expects us to use our heads, and to be alert and wise.

Escape out the Window

By the time David got home, Michal had already heard what had happened and knew that he had to leave. She let David down through a window and then put a household image in the bed, covered with a quilt of goat's hair. When Saul's messengers came to take David, Michal told them that he was sick. When Saul sent the messengers back to kill David in his bed, they found they had been tricked.

What happened next is almost unbelievable to me. Saul demanded of Michal, "Why have you deceived me? Why did you let my enemy go?" Because he backed her into a corner—into an impossible situation—she lied to him. She was trying to live with the man she loved, and her father was challenging her loyalty to her husband.

I have seven daughters and realize that I may also someday have seven sons-in-law. Basic to a proper relationship with them is my understanding that my daughters' first loyalty is to their husbands, and not to me.

After David got safely away from his house, he headed for Ramah, where Samuel lived. Somewhere along the way, he stopped to write a psalm, a prayer to God about his distress.

Deliver me from my enemies, O my God. . . .
And save me from men of bloodshed.
For behold, they have set an ambush for my life. . . .
For no guilt of mine, they run and set themselves against me. . . .
They return at evening, they howl like a dog,
And go around the city. . . .
They wander about for food,
And growl if they are not satisfied.
But as for me, I shall sing of Thy strength;
Yes, I shall joyfully sing of Thy lovingkindness in the morning,
For Thou has been my stronghold,
And a refuge in the day of my distress. (Psalm 59)

David with Samuel

With the turmoil in his life, David needed some encouragement, and he wisely went to see the faithful Prophet Samuel. David told Samuel everything Saul had done to him. It may have been during this visit that Samuel instructed David about the ordering of the temple services and worship to God that David instituted in later years. And Samuel must have reassured the young man that God had truly chosen him to be the king.

It is important for young people to have older friends who know God, and to whom they can go when they are in the stormy times of their lives. And it is also important that these older people of God realize their opportunity of ministering to troubled young people.

However, there was one thing that neither Samuel or David knew, and that was God's timetable. When we are in long and frustrating situations, we wish God would hurry. We even try to help Him. David still had many years to wait before he would become king, and it was a blessing that he didn't know it at this time.

Saul as Prophet

When Saul heard that David was with Samuel, he sent messengers to take him. However, when they came near and "saw the company of the prophets prophesying, with Samuel standing and presiding over them, the Spirit of God came upon the messengers of Saul; and they also prophesied" (1 Sam. 19:20). When Saul heard this, he sent another group, and then another, and the same thing happened.

Finally, Saul went up to Ramah. He found David, Samuel, and the prophets, and joined them in their prophesying. We are told that Saul also stripped off his clothes; but the word *stripped* refers to his outer garments, as does the word *naked*. All day and night he lay on the ground, prophesying. Whether he was only stripped to his underwear or naked as a jaybird, his appearance was unacceptable for the occasion. A naked man has very little credibility.

There had been one other time in Saul's life when he had prophesied until people began to ask what was wrong with him. At that time, it was in fulfillment of a prediction made by Samuel as a sign of Saul's anointing. It could have been now that, although Saul kept a safe distance from Samuel, he was trying to remind him of his kingship.

What Have I Done?

Again David fled from Saul—this time back to Jonathan. His question to his friend was, "What have I done? What is my iniquity? And what is my sin before your father, that he is seeking my life?"

As David took responsibility for his own behavior, he wondered if something he was doing was causing the rift between Saul and himself. When we have conflict and turmoil, it is wise to evaluate our own behavior to see if it offers an explanation for our trouble. It is not appropriate to assume that the fault necessarily lies with the other person.

If we live with an angry person, it is wise to consider the possibility that we are making that person angry. Tyrannical behavior is frequently the result of continual frustration. Modification of our behavior may well be necessary to lessen the turmoil.

Jonathan's response to David spoke of the closeness between father and son—"My father does nothing either great or small without disclosing it to me. So why should my father hide this thing from me? It is not so!" (20:2) David's answer was that Saul probably wouldn't want Jonathan to know that his close friend was in mortal danger, because he would be sad. "But truly as the Lord lives and as your soul lives, there is hardly a step between me and death" (v. 3).

The two devised a plan whereby they could find out the truth, but unfortunately their plan was based on a lie. Jonathan would tell his father that David had left the city to go to Bethlehem for a yearly sacrifice with his family. They assumed that Saul would then reveal his true feelings about David. David would be hiding in the field while Jonathan and his father were talking, and then Jonathan would come out and communicate with David, first by the shooting of arrows.

After they completed these arrangements, Jonathan made a covenant with the house of David, which was quite different from the covenant they had made when they first met. This new covenant looked ahead to the time when David would be king, when all his enemies would have been vanquished. Then they again vowed their personal love one to the other. Before he left David, Jonathan said, "As for the agreement of which you and I have spoken, behold, the Lord is between you and me forever" (20:23). A beautiful relationship between two exceptional young men!

Honesty

It bothers me that David and Jonathan devised a plan which included lies. In our home we have two rigid, nonnegotiable rules: You must obey, and you must not lie. The reason I feel so strongly about these rules is that human relationships are based on trust. We must not under any circumstances give our children the suggestion that we have lied to them. The effects of deception can be disastrous.

When telling the disciples about His Father's home, Jesus said, "If it were not so, I would have told you." As parents, we must teach our children with this same kind of certainty: *If a thing were not so, I would have told you.* Our children need to have absolute confidence in the honesty and integrity of their parents.

There is not a strict standard of truthfulness in our society. However, when a person lies or cheats, and does it long enough, he may come to the point where he can't determine what is true and what is false. Some people deceive the government because they feel too much is being taken away from them, or that it is not God's will that they be taxed. In my own case, when I have a problem with the government, I find it is really my problem, not God's. They may be taking too much of my money in taxes, but I don't think that can be spiritualized, nor can deception be an option.

We do not serve God by deceiving. As I live with my bride and our children, I have to be completely honest in all things, large and small. There is no justification for deception in the life of the believer.

David's Place at the Table

While David was hiding in the field, Saul noticed on the first day, and then on the second, that his place was empty at the table. He asked Jonathan why David had not appeared either day to eat with them. Jonathan told Saul the story about David going to be with his family in Bethlehem.

Someone might say that Jonathan was only repeating what David had said, but this is not the point. David did *not* beg leave of Jonathan to visit his family. Jonathan was deceiving his father as he described an action that had never taken place.

We may wonder why David, Michal, and Jonathan seemed to think it was necessary to lie to Saul. It is easy for us to say that they should have been direct and open with Saul, because we have not felt the consequences of Saul's personality. A more difficult question, though, we must ask ourselves. Are we the type of men and women who invite honesty and trust from our children, and from our friends and associates? Can they freely talk with us, even when they are hurting, or when they think they may hurt us by what they say?

Saul's reaction to David's whereabouts was indicative of the state of his inner soul. As his anger was kindled against Jonathan, from his mouth spewed out cruel words about both Jonathan and his mother. "You son of a perverse, rebellious woman! Do I not know that you are choosing the son of Jesse to your own shame and to the shame of your mother's nakedness? For as long as the son of Jesse lives on the earth, neither you nor your kingdom will be established. Therefore now, send and bring him to me, for he must surely die" (20:30-31).

If we try to imagine the rage and tone of voice in which all this was probably said, we set the scene for what happened next. Jonathan asked his father why David should die—what he had done. At this, Saul lost control of himself and hurled a spear at his own son, trying to kill him. Jonathan escaped and left the table in fierce anger, because he had been publicly dishonored by his father in front of the guests and servants of the royal household.

Farewell in the Field

Jonathan and David met in the fields for an emotional farewell. They both wept, especially David. American men have been told that "big boys don't cry." In my opinion, this is not healthy. David was freely expressing great sorrow for the terrible situation in Saul's family, which was his family also, and sorrow also at leaving his friend.

When it was time to go, Jonathan reminded David of their covenant in these words: "Go in safety, inasmuch as we have sworn to each other in the name of the Lord, saying, 'The Lord will be between me and you, and between my descendants and your descendants forever' " (20:42). Godly relationships withstand very unpleasant circumstances.

And Saul?

Saul had been chosen by God and given the Spirit of God. But because he would not be a person under authority, because he placed little value on the Word of God, the Lord gave up on him as king. But God did not give up on him as a person. Through Michal, Jonathan, and David, God tried to bring Saul to his senses. Typical of his personality, Saul would not yield—would not repent. He continued his slanderous, murderous attitudes toward the entire family.

Unfortunately, we sometimes see the same type of situation repeated today in professing Christian families. And it ought not to be so.

מָגֵן דָּוִד

3
Spiritual Compromise: Signs and Symptoms, Diagnosis and Treatment

1 SAMUEL 21—24

Every believer has potential for spiritual compromise, but few go as far as Saul did in open disobedience to God. The signs and symptoms of compromise in Saul's life were paranoia and ruthlessness. In the life of David, the signs of spiritual compromise included lying, fear, bizarre behavior, and living in ungodly surroundings.

Spiritual compromise is a sickness of the soul—a disease. As with a physical disease, so it is necessary to recognize signs and symptoms of a spiritual sickness, make correct diagnosis, and begin early treatment.

From Hero to Fugitive

David, national hero and son-in-law to the king, was now a fugitive. After saying farewell to his friend Jonathan, he made his way to the city of Nob, where Ahimelech the priest lived. When Ahimelech saw David, he fearfully asked, "Why are you alone and no one with you?" (21:1)

David lied to the priest. "The king has commissioned me with a matter, and has said to me, 'Let no one know anything about the matter on which I am sending you and with which I have commissioned you; and I have directed the young men to a certain place' " (21:2).

We can appreciate that he didn't want to blurt out, "My father-in-law is trying to kill me again." But this still gave him no excuse for lying.

David asked Ahimelech for food. Some loaves of bread, or whatever he had, would be all right. The priest told him that there was no ordinary bread available, but only that which had been consecrated as showbread. It could be eaten only by those under a vow. The loaves had been removed from the altar because new bread was being baked. David took the showbread in good conscience, and was considered then, and later, to have acted correctly in the situation.

Jesus spoke about the incident: "Have you not read what David did, when he became hungry, he and his companions; how he entered the house of God, and they ate the consecrated bread, which was not lawful for him to eat, nor for those with him, but for the priests alone?" (Matt. 12:3-4)

To Jesus, the consecration of the bread was not the issue, but whether David and his men were really hungry and in need. If they were, and Jesus said they were, then it was appropriate to eat the bread.

Jesus mentioned David because He had been criticized, along with His disciples, for gathering and eating grain on the Sabbath Day. Criticism is not necessarily a sign of spiritual compromise.

Possibly I am rationalizing here, but I would like to give a personal illustration of how a Christian could be misunderstood. Sunday afternoon is a block of time I have made available to spend with my family. Since my children are athletically inclined, we frequently play kickball or football in our front yard. Or we may play tennis together as a family.

Some people may feel that this is a poor use of the Lord's Day, but for me it is not. I have given this prayerful and careful thought. God knows my heart—and my feeling is that Sunday is a day of rest, and is appropriately spent relaxing with my children. We do this in our front yard because that is where we would play any other day of the week. Now if this playing time should extend into the Sunday evening worship time, I think it would be a compromising situation.

I know as Christians we are not to offend our brothers. However, I also know if I were overly concerned about what every other person might think, I would probably end up doing nothing! Fortunately, God knows my heart.

During this conversation about the showbread, a man named Doeg was standing by listening. He was an Edomite, and the chief herdsman for Saul. He was at the place of worship, "detained before the Lord," possibly for ceremonial purification. Doeg remembered well everything that he saw and heard, as we shall find out later. And David was fully aware that Doeg had heard all that was said.

One lie tends to lead to another. David needed a sword and asked Ahimelech, "Now, is there not a spear or a sword on hand? For I brought neither my sword nor my weapons with me, because the king's matter was urgent" (1 Sam. 21:8).

The priest answered, "The sword of Goliath the Philistine, whom you killed in the valley of Elah, behold, it is wrapped in a cloth behind the ephod; if you would take it for yourself, take it. For there is no other except it here."

David said, "There is none like it; give it to me" (21:9).

David then left the country and made his way to Gath, where Achish was the king. Apparently his reputation had traveled before him, for when he arrived in Gath the servants of the king accosted him and mocked him. We are not told so in 1 Samuel, but the title to Psalm 56 suggests that the servants seized him. While David was being held by them, he wrote:

Be gracious, O God, for man has trampled upon me. . . .
When I am afraid, I will put my trust in Thee. . . .
What can mere man do to me? All day long
they distort my words; All their thoughts are
against me for evil. They attack, they lurk,
they watch my steps, as they have waited to take my life. . . .
Thou hast taken account of my wanderings;
Put my tears in Thy bottle; are they not in Thy book? . . .
For Thou hast delivered my soul from death, indeed
my feet from stumbling, so that I may walk before God
In the light of the living.

This psalm contrasts with 1 Samuel 21. David's sense of fear may have grown as he was detained, for we read of a plan to escape from Gath. David decided that it would be particularly offensive to King Achish if he feigned insanity. The reason for this is suggested in the king's response to what David did: "Do I lack madmen, that you have brought this one to act the madman in my presence? Shall this one come into my house?" (21:15)

Achish must have had insane people in his own household, and one more around was just too much. David was behaving insanely before him, scribbling on the doors of the gate, even letting saliva run down into his beard. Jewish men were particularly proud of their beards, tending to groom them very carefully. When Achish was convinced of David's insanity and allowed him to leave, David made his way to the cave of Adullam.

We have just seen David telling lies, and fearful to the point that he became a fugitive from his own land. As a stranger in another land, he masqueraded as insane because of fear. These are not the signs of a man living in close touch with God. Rather they are symptoms of compromise. As we look at David, we need to look into our own lives to see if there are similar signs and symptoms of spiritual compromise.

After David had been set free and had left Gath, he composed a beautiful psalm, one difficult to associate with his masquerade of madness.

I will bless the Lord at all times;
His praise shall continually be in my mouth.

My soul shall make its boast in the Lord;
The humble shall hear it and rejoice;
O magnify the Lord with me,
And let us exalt His name together.
I sought the Lord, and He answered me,
And delivered me from all my fears (Psalm 34:1-4).

David in the Cave of Adullam

After David had settled in the cave of Adullam, the members of his family heard that he was there and traveled down to be with him. Other people came too, making a rather motley crew: "Everyone who was in distress, and everyone who was in debt, and everyone who was discontented, gathered to him; and he became captain over them. Now there were about 400 men with him" (1 Sam. 22:2).

Today there are people in distress, in debt, and in discontent. Don't ever apologize for a Christian who is struggling. Don't ever feel ashamed of a friend who has failed. Hold that friend up in prayer because God can triumph, and your friend can be drawn to the church and to fellow Christians. Not many wise or mighty or noble, by human standards, are called into the family of God. (See 1 Cor. 1:26-29.)

Being alone in your trouble is one thing. But when people join themselves to you, almost as an announcement of your difficulties, there is no way to deny your situation. As the reality of David's distress seemed to close in on him, he expressed the pain of his exile:

I pour out my complaint before Him;
I declare my trouble before Him.
When my spirit was overwhelmed within me,
Thou didst know my path.
In the way where I walk, they have hidden a trap for me.
Look to the right and see; for there is no one who regards me;
There is no escape for me; no one cares for my soul.
I cried out to Thee, O Lord; I said, "Thou art my refuge,
My portion in the land of the living." Give heed to my cry,
For I am brought very low (Psalm 142).

To Moab and Back to Judah

David was soon on the move again, this time to Moab. You will remember that he had Moabite blood in him through his ancestress Ruth. David said to the king of Moab, "Please let my father and mother come and stay with you until I know what God will do for me" (1 Sam. 22:3). The king granted them refuge for the time that David was in the stronghold.

While he was in Moab, David was visited by the Prophet Gad who said to him, "Get back where you belong, David. Go to Judah." One thing I admire so much in David is that he had an obedient heart. He asked himself, *What does God want me to do?* When the prophet came along and said, "Get back in Judah with God's people," David immediately did so.

However, obedience did not solve all of David's problems. God never promised anyone that he would "live happily ever after." Obedience is not necessarily rewarded by a blissful, trouble-free life.

Saul, Doeg, and the Priests

The story now shifts back to Saul, whose spiritual compromise was far more serious than David's. Saul was exhibiting paranoia as well as ruthlessness, indicating the depth of his compromise.

Saul was living in his hometown, Gibeah. As he sat under a tree surrounded by his fellow Benjaminites, news arrived that David was back in Judah. As Saul thought about the threat to his throne, he said to his tribesmen: "Will the son of Jesse also give to all of you fields and vineyards? Will he make you all commanders of thousands and commanders of hundreds? For all of you have conspired against me so that there is no one who discloses to me when my son makes a covenant with the son of Jesse, and there is none of you who is sorry for me or discloses to me that my son has stirred up my servant against me to lie in ambush, as it is this day" (22:7-8).

Not only was Saul sitting in idleness, but he showed signs of paranoia, for he felt that everyone was against him with conspirators on every side. This was a sign of serious spiritual compromise.

Doeg the Edomite, Saul's herdsman, was anxious to demonstrate his loyalty to Saul. He reported, "I saw the son of Jesse coming to Nob, to Ahimelech the son of Ahitub" (22:9). And he went on to relate the story of David eating the showbread and taking Goliath's sword.

Saul promptly called Ahimelech to him. Then he also called the priest's relatives, and all the other priests who lived in Nob. Saul asked him, "Why have you and the son of Jesse conspired against me? (22:13) Notice the paranoia, extending even to the priest.

Ahimelech answered Saul, "Who among all your servants is as faithful as David, even the king's son-in-law, who is captain over your guard, and is honored in your house? Did I just begin to inquire of God for him today? Far be it from me! Do not let the king impute anything to his servant or to any of the household of my father, for your servant knows nothing at all of this whole affair" (22:14-15).

Saul's answer was one of ruthlessness, another sign of severe compromise. "You shall surely die, Ahimelech, you and all your father's household!" (22:16) It seems incredible that Saul would murder all the priests; according to Doeg, only Ahimelech was involved with David. But Saul was so paranoid that he wasn't thinking straight.

The king turned to his footmen and ordered them to slay the priests of the Lord, but they would not obey their king. They were not willing "to put forth their hands to attack the priests of the Lord" (22:17).

However, Doeg was standing conveniently by, so Saul suggested that he kill the priests. The Edomite turned and attacked, killing 85 priests. Then he traveled to Nob and killed everyone in the city except one person, Abiathar the son of Ahimelech, who escaped and fled to David.

This slaughter seems to be a second fulfillment of a prophecy made to Eli, that no old man would remain in his house. Eli and his sons were killed, leaving only an infant male, Ichabod. Now the only male priest left was Abiathar, a young man. (See 1 Sam. 2:30-31; 4:11-22.)

The Price of Compromise

When Abiathar reached David and told him of the killings, David replied, "I knew on that day, when Doeg the Edomite was there, that he would surely tell Saul. I have brought about the death of every person in your father's household. Stay with me, do not be afraid, for he who seeks my life seeks your life; for you are safe with me" (22:22-23).

Scholars believe that David wrote the words of Psalm 52 to express his sorrow for the people of Nob, and his anger at Doeg.

Why do you boast in evil, O mighty man? . . .
Your tongue devises destruction,
Like a sharp razor, O worker of deceit. . . .
But God will break you down forever;
He will snatch you up, and tear you away from your tent,
And uproot you from the land of the living. . . .

David had to live with the fact that he had caused the death of 85 priests. How could the Word of God be more clear about the tragedy of compromise? God expects us to obey Him.

However, David maintained his confidence in God and took responsibility for Abiathar at this difficult time. God would not permit David to fall apart at the seams.

In difficult times we don't give up, but go forward because our strength is in God and not in ourselves. This is especially important when we have failed. The love and mercy of God are all sufficient. Although we are unfaithful, God is never unfaithful. As children of the Almighty God, we can go forward with great confidence. Although life may not be all we want it to be, we know God can bring into our lives the things He wants us to experience. For the believer, there is always the road beyond. God is never through with us, no matter what we do. "His lovingkindness is everlasting" (Ps. 106:1).

David and the People of Keilah

How does God deal with a compromising Christian? He brings into his life circumstances and opportunities that will take him through his sense of failure and strengthen him.

For David the circumstance was the plight of the city of Keilah.

Someone came to David and said, "Behold, the Philistines are fighting against Keilah, and are plundering the threshing floors" (1 Sam. 23:1). After the cultivating during the growing season, after the intense labor of the harvesttime when the grain was into the threshing floor, the enemy came.

When David heard this he inquired of the Lord, "Shall I go and attack these Philistines?" And the Lord said, "Go and attack them and deliver Keilah." Even though David had failed, he confidently turned to God in prayer, and God answered him clearly and specifically. Our heavenly Father is a God of judgment, but He is also a God of love and understanding. He knows our weaknesses, our areas of compromise. He is fully aware of everything that happens in our lives, and He does not turn His back on us.

One day when I was driving one of my teenage daughters to school, she and I got into a tense discussion, after which there was a long silence. As we reached the high school, she said, "Dad." I thought, *Oh, she is going to apologize for the way she behaved.*

"Dad, could I have a dollar for lunch?"

As I was digging into my pocket to find a dollar for her, I looked over at her eyes and saw that they were literally dancing and twinkling. She said, "I left my lunch at home." I gave her the dollar, she leaped from the car, and said, "Thanks, Dad," and was gone.

Now, if I as a short-tempered, earthly father can hand a dollar to a daughter with whom I have just had a tense discussion, how much greater is the love and patience of God! He is our heavenly Father. We may have some tense discussions with Him and feel very angry with Him, because we think He doesn't understand us. But when we need Him, He is always there, ready to lead us on in love, and to comfort us in our times of failure.

Prayerful Leadership

David told his 400 men of God's command to deliver the city of Keilah, and they discussed this plan among themselves. We must remember that these were the discontents and the debtors, not exactly outstanding citizens. They were fearful even in Judah, let alone fighting the Philistines. So they came to their leader and said, "You want us to go and fight the Philistines but we'd rather not. We're scared."

What did David do? He didn't say, "Listen, I'm your leader. Do what I tell you."

Not at all. Instead, he went back to God and said, "Father, did I get those signals straight? The people with me are a bit concerned about what I think You want us to do."

I like to have this type of prayerful thought. I like to think about things, trusting that God will guide my thoughts. Once I make a decision, it is not uncommon for me later to ask, "Did I make the right decision?" My confidence is not in the decision, which may seem right or wrong at the moment, but rather in the fact that the decision has been made in a prayerful manner. I believe decisions made in the counsel of God are always in the will of God.

You and I can go to God and say, "Now, Father, my understanding is that You want me to do this, but I need a little assurance that this is really what You want." If you quietly wait upon God, there will come a sense of peace and understanding that this is—or is not—what God wants you to do. This happened to David. God said, "Arise, go down to Keilah, for I will give the Philistines into your hand" (22:4). And this is exactly what happened, for David and his men delivered the people of Keilah from the Philistines.

The Ephod

In 1 Samuel 23:6 we have a parenthesis. When Abiathar, son of Ahimelech, came to be with David, he brought with him the ephod used by the high priest. This ephod was a garment of gold, blue, purple, crimson, and twisted linen. Its pieces were held together by two onyx stones, each engraved with the names of six tribes of Israel. When the priest inquired of God, two words which were probably on the stones, *Urim* and *Thummin,* were attached to or inside of his breastplate. In some manner, God indicated His will for the people. *Urim* and *Thummin* literally mean "lights and perfections."

When Moses first robed Aaron in his garments, "he then placed the breastpiece on him, and in the breastpiece he put the Urim and the Thummin" (Lev. 8:8). In the Book of Ezra, we read that the people were not to eat from "the most holy things until a priest stood up with Urim and Thummin" (2:63). When God told Moses how to install Joshua as leader of the people, He said, "Moreover, he shall stand before Eleazar, the priest, who shall inquire for him by the judgment of the Urim before the Lord" (Num. 27:21). David was soon going to need that ephod.

David and the People of Keilah Again
When Saul found out that David had delivered the people of Keilah and was still in the area, he interpreted it to mean that God was delivering David into his hands. Keilah was a city with double gates and bars. Saul, with ruthless intention, summoned his men and they marched toward Keilah, thinking that David was cornered. It seems incredible that Saul felt God was working on his behalf, especially when we see no evidence that Saul had repented.

David realized that Saul had ulterior motives, and asked Abiathar to bring the ephod, as he asked guidance from God in prayer. David knew that Saul was coming to Keilah to destroy the city because of him, and he asked the Lord, "Will the men of Keilah surrender me into his hand? Will Saul come down just as Thy servant has heard? O Lord God of Israel, I pray, tell Thy servant. And the Lord said, 'He will come down.' Then David said, 'Will the men of Keilah surrender me and my men into the hands of Saul?' And the Lord said, 'They will surrender you'" (1 Sam. 23:11-12).

When the chips were down, the people of Keilah were going to save their own skins. It didn't seem to matter that David had just rescued them and their harvest from the Philistines.

We could say, "That ought not to be." Well, I have lived more than 50 years, and all I can say is, "Yes, they will deliver him up." That is human nature. When people are under stress, they tend to look out for themselves and forget what others have done for them.

Is this true of Christians as well as non-Christians? I think it is. Surely, Christians ought to live differently. But my experience has been that they usually do not. The Lord had told David just what was going to happen. The Word of God does not white-wash situations. Self-preservation is a characteristic of the people of God, as well as of the people of the world.

David and his men, now 600 in number, left Keilah and went in all directions. When Saul heard of their escape, he gave up the pursuit.

David in the Wilderness

Some time elapsed before Saul began the pursuit again. David and his men were now in the wilderness of Ziph, and Saul was seeking him every day. During this time of wilderness hide-and-seek, Jonathan managed to visit David to encourage him in the Lord. He said to David, "Do not be afraid, because the hand of Saul my father shall not find you, and you will be king over Israel and I will be next to you; and Saul my father knows that also" (23:17).

Do you relate to people as Jonathan did? Do you know a troubled Christian? A compromising Christian? Then go to that person, not to strengthen him in his own way, but to strengthen and encourage him in the Lord. This should be your motive and prayer.

After they had made a covenant, Jonathan went back to his home. Now it might seem strange that he would not stay with David. But we have to remember that Jonathan, as the son of King Saul, had an allegiance to his father. Because Saul was determined to find David, Jonathan might have found himself fighting against his own father. I think that would have been unbearable to a man of Jonathan's caliber.

I have tried to teach my children to honor their father and mother, even though they might think that either parent is not behaving honorably at the time. I have tried to admonish my children to realize that their parents are more important than their friends. I believe Jonathan's priorities were correct when he went to his house, rather than staying with David.

During this time in the wilderness, David composed psalms to God. One of the most expressive of a person's need for God is Psalm 63.

O God, Thou art my God; I shall seek Thee earnestly;
My soul thirsts for Thee, my flesh yearns for Thee,
In a dry and weary land where there is no water.
Thus I have beheld Thee in the sanctuary,
To see Thy power and Thy glory. . . .
My soul clings to Thee; Thy right hand upholds me.
But those who seek my life, to destroy it,
Will go into the depths of the earth. . . .

David and the People of Ziph

David was out in the wilderness when the people of the town of
Ziph heard that his 600 men were trying to hide there. The
Ziphites sent word to Saul, telling him that David was hiding in
the forest, and suggesting that the king come down so that they
could surrender David into Saul's hands. Saul's response was again
incredible: "May you be blessed of the Lord; for you have had
compassion on me" (1 Sam. 23:21). Then Saul told them to send
people out to determine exactly where David was. He was re-
luctant to play hide-and-seek in the wilderness any longer.

Saul was still spiritually oriented in his language, though he
was obviously out of fellowship with God. I say *obviously*, because there is no way a believer can honestly spiritualize his words,
when deep in his heart he knows he is planning to break one of
God's commandments.

David had moved to the wilderness of Maon, but Saul found
him there. Saul had his army on one side of the mountain, and
David had his army on the other side. David was fearful and
trying to escape, but Saul and his men surrounded David's small
army.

We can sympathize with David's fear. It looked as if he was
in a hopeless situation. However, God was in control. A messenger
came to Saul saying, "Hurry and come, for the Philistines have
made a raid on the land" (23:27). Saul had to discontinue his
pursuit of David in order to fight the Philistines.

How many times in your life have you felt totally surrounded
by circumstances, only to see God step in and resolve the problem with no effort whatsoever on your part? If you have not had

this experience, you will. For God uses this strategy frequently in the lives of His children. He wants us to have confidence in all circumstances, that His purpose will prevail.

David at Engedi

David, now free to move, went to the strongholds at Engedi. After Saul had finished fighting the Philistines, he was informed of David's position. Saul took 3,000 men from all Israel "and went to seek David and his men in front of the Rocks of the Wild Goats" (24:2). How about those odds—3,000 chosen men against David's motley crew of 600? But God was very much aware of the situation.

In the meantime, David and his men were hiding in a cave, hoping the king would pass on by. But Saul went inside that very cave.

David's men thought the Lord had brought David's enemy right to them. They sat in the inner recesses of the large cave and discussed what they should do next. David's men said to him, "Behold, this is the day of which the Lord said to you, 'Behold, I am about to give your enemy into your hand, and you shall do to him as it seems good to you' " (24:4).

That was a logical conclusion on their part, but David's mind and heart heard something quite different. He arose, and very quietly cut off a portion of Saul's robe. Afterward, David's conscience bothered him, and he said, "Far be it from me because of the Lord that I should do this thing to my lord, the Lord's anointed, to stretch out my hand against him, since he is the Lord's anointed" (24:6). Also David restrained his servants from attacking Saul. Finally, Saul left the cave and went on his way.

Despite the fact that David had been a victim of Saul's anger for a long time, he would not take advantage of the king. David, recognizing that Saul was the anointed of God, refused to harm him. He was also penitent because he had cut Saul's robe.

There are people in our lives who are the anointed of God. I believe that all pastors, elders, and Sunday School teachers are anointed of the Lord. We must be very careful not to embarrass them, or harm them in any way. To a certain extent, our spouses and children are the anointed of the Lord in our lives, too. When they are in very vulnerable situations, we are to guard them from any harm.

As you think of some of these people in your life, you may be saying, "They don't act like the anointed of the Lord." Do you think Saul did? David's conscience bothered him because he had embarrassed Saul. We all need this kind of sensitivity to the people in our lives.

David and Saul

After Saul had walked away from the cave, David went outside and called, "My lord the king!" When Saul looked behind him, "David bowed with his face to the ground and prostrated himself" (24:8). Then David said to Saul, "Why do you listen to people who tell you that I am trying to harm you?"

> Behold, this day your eyes have seen that the Lord had given you today into my hand in the cave, and some said to kill you, but my eye had pity on you; and I said, "I will not stretch out my hand against my lord, for he is the Lord's anointed."
>
> Now, my father, see! Indeed, see the edge of your robe in my hand! For in that I cut off the edge of your robe and did not kill you, know and perceive that there is no evil or rebellion in my hands, and I have not sinned against you, though you are lying in wait for my life to take it.
>
> May the Lord judge between you and me, and may the Lord avenge me on you; but my hand shall not be against you. As the proverb of the ancients says, "Out of the wicked comes forth wickedness"; but my hand shall not be against you. After whom has the king of Israel come out? . . . A dead dog, a single flea? The Lord therefore be judge and decide between you and me; and may He see and plead my cause, and deliver me from your hand (24:10-15).

We must realize the embarrassment that Saul felt in front of his men. He had been very vulnerable inside that cave and totally unaware of his danger. Furthermore, David had given clear evidence that he did not wish to harm Saul.

Saul's response gives us a bit of hope for this disobedient man of God. "Is this your voice, my son David?" (24:16) And Saul wept.

Then he said to David,

You are more righteous than I; for you have dealt well with me, while I have dealt wickedly with you. And you have declared today that you have done good to me, that the Lord delivered me into your hand and yet you did not kill me. For if a man finds his enemy, will he let him go away safely? May the Lord therefore reward you with good in return for what you have done to me this day. And now, behold, I know that you shall surely be king, and that the kingdom of Israel shall be established in your hand. So now swear to me by the Lord that you will not cut off my descendants after me, and that you will not destroy my name from my father's household (24:17-21).

David did swear the oath that Saul requested and each man went his own way. It sounds as if Saul was sincerely repenting. He recognized that David was in fact more righteous than he, and would be his successor. But typical of a man like Saul, he asked that David would not cut off his family in the future. David must have picked up this aspect of Saul's confession, because he proceeded to a stronghold. He was not about to carry this reconciliation to a point of further danger. If you have a conflict like this in your life, it is good not to force the situation. David knew Saul, and he didn't expect too much. He defended himself against the attacks of Saul; he wasn't just going to stand there and be killed. But he would not raise his hand to harm Saul in any way. We all need this type of balance in our lives.

מָגֵן דָּוִד

4
Anger and Retaliation

1 SAMUEL 25—26

I happen to have the rather long nickname of "Painless Paul, the Patient's Pal." My patients' casts are signed P.P.P.P. Now I won't bore you with the story of how I got that name, but I will admit that no one has ever called me "Patient Paul." I can relate easily to David's tendency toward impatience and anger.

In this story we will see David so violently angry that he was ready to murder a man who would not comply with his request. You may understand how David felt. Many people in our society experience similar feelings of anger and vengeance. And these same people often consult their doctors with such symptoms as high blood pressure, stomach ulcers, colitis, and even hives.

Feelings of retaliation and vengeance are much like cancer in that they can literally eat away at the patient. The angry person who desires retaliation suffers far more than the person with whom he is angry.

In the Sermon on the Mount, Jesus taught us to turn the other cheek, to go the extra mile, to yield our coats and cloaks, rather than retaliate. There is no room for vengeance in a Christian's personality. In the Book of Hebrews we read, " 'Vengeance is Mine, I shall repay,' saith the Lord of Hosts" (10:30).

Causes for David's Anger

David had been running from Saul for a long time. This type of stress takes its toll on the human personality. In 1 Samuel 25:1 we read that Samuel died. The Prophet Samuel had been a spiritual father to David, and while all Israel went to Ramah to bury him, David went to the Wilderness of Paran, the place where the Children of Israel had wandered for 40 years. There he was alone with his sorrow, unable to share it with the people of God.

Frustration at Saul, sorrow about Samuel—and then a man named Nabal came into the picture. "There was a man in Maon whose business was in Carmel; and the man was very rich, and he had 3,000 sheep and 1,000 goats." Nabal also had a wife, Abigail, who was "intelligent and beautiful in appearance, but the man was harsh and evil in his dealings" (25:2-3).

Nabal was a descendant of Caleb, who had been a friend of Joshua and a great man of God. This clearly suggests that one's spiritual heritage does not necessarily lead to godly offspring. There are no grandchildren in the kingdom of God.

David heard that Nabal was shearing his sheep and he sent some of his young men to Carmel to ask for payment for the services his men had rendered to Nabal. To care for 4,000 animals required many men, and David's band had given protection to these shepherds and their animals. We might at first consider this a shakedown scheme, but David's claims were legitimate.

Now, when Nabal would be selling the wool and some prepared animals, David sent his men to ask for a portion of the profits. They were to say,

Have a long life, peace be to you, and peace be to your house, and peace be to all that you have. And now I have heard that you have shearers; now your shepherds have been with us and we have not insulted them, nor have they missed anything all the days they were in Carmel. Ask your young men and they will tell you. Therefore let my young men find favor in your eyes, for we have come on a festive day. Please give whatever you find at hand to your servants and to your son David (25:6-8).

There is a lesson in this—wealthy people are not necessarily the most generous people. It seems that they get caught in the trap of "keeping their money working for them." Often they have little cash at hand. David's approach was correct in not asking for a specific sum of money. Fund raisers should take note. It seems more appropriate to invite a wealthy man to contribute as his heart directs, rather than to stipulate the amount he should give.

Nabal responded, "Who is David? And who is the son of Jesse? There are many servants today who are each breaking away from his master. Shall I then take my bread and my water and my meat that I have slaughtered for my shearers, and give it to men whose origin I do not know?" (25:10-11) It is almost certain that Nabal knew who David was. After all, they lived in a small country and David was a national hero, their most famous soldier.

David's young men reported Nabal's response to David, and got an answer typical of this fiery military man: "Each of you gird on his sword" (25:13). David took 400 of his men, all of them armed, to punish Nabal. Their intent was to kill every male in the household.

Decisions

One of Nabal's shepherds heard the exchange between Nabal and David's men and went to inform Abigail, Nabal's wife. He told her that Nabal had railed at the young men; and he verified that David's men had, in fact, been protective of the shepherds.

The men were very good to us, and we were not insulted, nor did we miss anything as long as we went about with them, while we were in the fields. They were a wall to us both by night and by day, all the time we were with them tending the sheep. Now therefore, know and consider what you should do, for evil is plotted against our master and against all his household; and he is such a worthless man that no one can speak to him (25:15-17).

We have said that Saul was the type of man who made his own children feel uncomfortable in speaking the truth to him. Nabal apparently was the same kind of man, for his servant realized that no one could speak to him. The implication was that Abigail could not suggest to Nabal what he should do either. Gentlemen, this should challenge us to consider our own personalities, and our relationships to our families, to insure that we are not the type of men who cannot be approached in honesty and truth by those closest to us.

Abigail quickly took 200 loaves of bread, 2 jugs of wine, 5 sheep already prepared, 5 measures of roasted grain, 100 clusters of raisins, 200 cakes of figs, and loaded all this on several donkeys. She then told her young men to go on before her to meet David.

David, traveling toward Carmel, had said, "Surely in vain I have guarded all that this man has in the wilderness, so that nothing was missed of all that belonged to him; and he has returned me evil for good. May God do so to the enemies of David, and more also, if by morning I leave as much as one male of any who belong to him" (25:21-22).

David still had murder on his mind. If an angry person realizes that he is planning to break one of the commandments of God because of his anger, he knows that his motives and plans are not of God. There is no way to rationalize this type of behavior.

Abigail and David

"When Abigail saw David, she hurried and dismounted from her donkey, and fell on her face before David, and bowed herself to the ground. And she fell at his feet and said, 'On me alone, my lord, be the blame. And please let your maidservant speak to you, and listen to the words of your maidservant' " (25:23-24).

Ladies, if you have an angry man on your hands, this is a good lesson to learn. It may sound chauvinistic, but a soft, slow answer turns away wrath. Abigail, following the oriental custom of bowing before the male, was making it abundantly clear to David that she had great respect for him. I think an angry man should be approached in the same respectful way by a woman of today.

Abigail's next statement strongly discredited her husband.

Please do not let my lord pay attention to this worthless man, Nabal, for as his name is, so is he. Nabal is his name and folly is with him; but I your maidservant did not see the young men of my lord whom you sent.

Now therefore, my lord, as the Lord lives, and as your soul lives, since the Lord has restrained you from shedding blood, and from avenging yourself by your own hand, now then let your enemies, and those who seek evil against my lord, be as Nabal. And now let this gift which your maidservant has brought to my lord be given to the young men who accompany my lord (25:25-27).

While Abigail was seemingly discrediting her husband, she was certainly speaking the truth about him. And she did seem to have a sincere concern that David not take vengeance into his own hands—an action inappropriate for a servant of God.

I personally admire the young man who recognized the danger of the situation and then reported it to Abigail. He was assuming responsibility and using good judgment. I also respond to Abigail for recognizing the problem and taking quick action on behalf of her household. Because Nabal was such a churlish man, the people who saw the problem and felt responsibility about it had to do something to prevent a mass slaughter. And there are times today when we must circumvent the usual chain of command, where an employee must speak up, or a wife must take action, to avoid a calamity, and to protect innocent people from the unreasoning wrath of tyrants like Nabal.

As Abigail continued to speak to David, she expressed great insight and intelligence in her words. Assuming full responsibility for Nabal's act, she asked David a second time to forgive her. And then she spoke of David's own future, bringing out the following points:

- God will establish your family.
- No calamity will overtake you.
- God will wrap up your life and put it with His own treasure, but the lives of your enemies He will throw like stones from a sling.
- You don't want your future courage to falter because of bad conscience over anger or innocent bloodshed.
- When God does all this, you will remember me. (See 25:28-31.)

Again we see why David was a man after God's heart. He responded to Abigail: "Blessed be the Lord God of Israel, who sent you this day to meet me, and blessed be your discernment, and blessed be you, who have kept me this day from bloodshed, and from avenging myself by my own hand" (25:32-33).

Again I may sound chauvinistic, but I find it remarkable that this valiant man of war would listen to a woman. That simply was not the custom of those days. Some might think that because of David's eye for a pretty woman, he was listening to Abigail. But the dress of that day was long robes and veils, so that he wasn't seeing that much of her beauty.

God prepared Abigail to be in the right place at the right time, to prevent David from making a very serious error, one that would affect his reign as second king of Israel. God has a plan for every believer's life, and prepares that person to fulfill His plan, in obedience.

After David accepted the gifts which Abigail had brought to him, he said to her, "Go up to your house in peace. See, I have listened to you and granted your request" (25:35).

In Abigail David had met a very strong and very intelligent woman. However, I don't find her strength unusual. I happen to believe that women are generally stronger emotionally than men. Most men have known this for a long time. But women need to realize it. Their influence over husbands and children is profound. One reason for this influence is a woman's tremendous ability to love. In my opinion, the love of a woman is second only to the love of God.

The old saying, "The hand that rocks the cradle rules the

world," is more true than we want to admit. Behind most successful men are good women. Behind many fallen men are bad women.

In the Book of Ephesians, the Apostle Paul pointed out that a woman was to be submissive to her husband in everything. Yet prior to that, he stated that we are all to be submissive to one another, and that means the husband to the wife, as well as the other way around. The two are one flesh. I believe that Paul emphasized the submission of the woman to her husband because a man has a great need for support from a loving mate.

I see the male ego as a weakness, not as a strength. Male aggressiveness is often a cover-up for a man's sense of insecurity. We know that little boys grow up to be big boys who happen to be in men's bodies. I find it humorous during televised football games to see professional players who look at the camera and say, "Hi, Mom!" The need a man has for a good woman in his life is tremendous. Unfortunately, there are men who deny this need and behave with surliness and irresponsibility toward family members, as well as toward other people. This behavior places great strain on their wives and children. This seems to have been Abigail's situation.

Nabal's Death

Abigail returned home to find her husband holding a feast fit for a king. Since he was very drunk, she decided to wait until morning to speak to him about her encounter with David. When she did tell him, "his heart died within him so that he became as a stone" (v. 37). About 10 days later, "the Lord struck Nabal, and he died" (v. 38). Medical details in this story are interesting to me. Some people have thought that Nabal suffered a stroke, but it seems consistent with medical experience that he had a heart attack, a coronary thrombosis. An acute coronary can cause a person to fall into a state which would seem stonelike. Such a patient can be in shock, cold and clammy, and with so little strength that he can hardly move a muscle. Also it is not uncommon for the victim of a coronary to expire about 10 days after the onset of the attack.

David's response to the news of Nabal's death was, "Blessed be the Lord, who has pleaded the cause of my reproach from the hand of Nabal, and has kept back His servant from evil. The Lord has also returned the evildoing of Nabal on his own head" (v. 39).

David recognized that God had not only prevented him from committing murder, but had permanently removed Nabal from the scene, and through natural causes. David was also grateful to Abigail for her role in this episode in his life. So grateful, in fact, that after the appropriate time of mourning, he sent a proposal of marriage to her. She accepted, prepared herself, and came to him to become his wife. David was also married to Ahinoam of Jezreel. His first wife, Michal, was now with another husband, since her father, Saul, had given her in marriage to Palti, the son of Laish, of Gallim.

The maliciousness of Saul is so apparent. Michal had truly loved David, and now she belonged to another man. We remember that David had first been engaged to Merab and that Saul had married her to another man before David came back from war. What happens to a man that motivates him to deal so unkindly with his own flesh and blood—with his own daughters?

Saul and David Again

As 1 Samuel 26 begins, the Ziphites were reporting to Saul that David was hiding in the wilderness of Ziph, on the hill of Hachilah. So Saul took 3,000 men down to the wilderness to search for David.

In this story, which is almost a repeat of one in chapter 23, we see David's unwillingness to lay his hand upon the anointed of God. This is a lesson every Christian needs to learn. God is controlling every aspect of our lives. His anointed ones are brought into our lives for a purpose. Thus, we have no need for vengeance or retaliation in our hearts.

When David realized that Saul was seeking him again, he sent spies out to discover Saul's location. As David and his men approached the place where Saul's soldiers were, David turned to Ahimelech and Abishai asking which of them would go with him to Saul's camp that night. Abishai answered, "I will go down with you."

The two men went that night and found Saul and all his men asleep. Saul's spear was stuck in the ground beside his head, and he was lying in a slit trench.

Abishai wanted to kill Saul instantly and get it over with. He didn't want to mutilate him, but just finish him off with one stroke. David could have felt tempted to spiritualize the situation. For Abishai had said, "God has delivered him into your hand." *God is on your side, David; He has made Saul vulnerable. Now you can solve your problems.*

We must be careful in difficult times not to spiritualize and rationalize ourselves into doing harm to another person—all in the name of God.

David's reply was similar to when he had encountered Saul in the cave:

Who can stretch out his hand against the Lord's anointed and be without guilt? . . . As the Lord lives, surely the Lord will strike him, or his day will come that he dies, or he will go down into battle and perish. The Lord forbid that I should stretch out my hand against the Lord's anointed; but now please take the spear that is at his head and the jug of water, and let us go (26:9-11).

They took Saul's spear and the water jug and turned to leave. But notice that they didn't rattle the two together. You don't tempt God. You don't jump off a pinnacle and expect the angels to protect you. You don't make yourself vulnerable to the point of being foolish. Saul's men were asleep, and after David was a safe distance away from them, he called back to Abner:

Will you not answer, Abner? . . . Are you not a man? And who is like you in Israel? Why then have you not guarded your lord the king? For one of the people came to destroy the king your lord. This thing that you have done is not good. As the Lord lives, all of you must surely die, because you did not guard your lord, the Lord's anointed. And now, see where the king's spear is, and the jug of water that was at his head (26:14-16).

Saul recognized David's voice and called, "Is this your voice, my son David?" And David said, "It is my voice, my lord the king."

Then David asked Saul,

Why then is my lord pursuing his servant? For what have I done? Or what evil is in my hand? Now, therefore, please let my lord the king listen to the words of his servant. If the Lord has stirred you up against me, let Him accept an offering; but if it is men, cursed are they before the Lord, for they have driven me out today that I should have no attachment with the inheritance of the Lord, saying, "Go, serve other gods" (26:17-19).

The phrase "the inheritance of the Lord" refers to the people of God. Because of Saul, David could have no place with his own people. Except for Abiathar the priest who was with him, he had no structured religious life. He couldn't even attend the funeral of Samuel.

David also suggested to Saul that he examine the source of his information, whether he was getting it from God or man. This is a wise bit of advice for us today. Check your sources before you believe something for sure. In your home, if one child tells you something against another, talk to that other one too, and get the whole story. It is amazing how much variation there can be in the same story as told by two people.

Then David asked that Saul not let him die apart from the people of God. He suggested that Saul had come as king to look for a single flea, just as a hunter pursues a partridge.

Again Saul declared his sin, and asked David to return home. "I will not harm you again because my life was precious in your sight this day. Behold, I have played the fool and have committed a serious error" (26:21).

David responded by asking the king to send one of his men to fetch the spear and water jug. And he repeated his refusal to touch the anointed of the Lord.

And the Lord will repay each man for his righteousness and his faithfulness; for the Lord delivered you into my hand today, but I refused to stretch out my hand against the Lord's anointed.

Now behold, as your life was highly valued in my sight this day, so may my life be highly valued in the sight of the Lord, and may He deliver me from all distress.

"Then Saul said to David, 'Blessed are you, my son David; you will both accomplish much and surely prevail.' So David went on his way and Saul returned to his place" (vv. 23-25).

This would seem an appropriate time for the sun to set in the West, and for the main characters to live happily ever after. But that is not the case. Rather David was entering into a very depressed time of his life, and drifting away from the will of God.

מָגֵן דָּוִד

5
Discouraged, Depressed, and Out of the Will of God

1 SAMUEL 27—31

David had become discouraged and depressed from the long cat-and-mouse game with Saul. He had heard Saul openly repent and declare that he was discontinuing his pursuit of David, only to hear later that the king was after him again.

It is not uncommon for a person to become depressed after a trying set of circumstances. In medical school I saw this, as students experienced "post-exam depression" following months of intense study and the pressure of finals. Fortunately, it was usually short-lived.

Few of us are as volcanic and complex as David. His depression was the result of many years of difficulty, and it finally reached such a depth that he fled to the Philistines, where he lived more than a year, plundering, murdering, and even planning to march against the people of God.

What's the Use?

"David said to himself, 'Now I will perish one day by the hand of Saul. There is nothing better for me than to escape into the land of the Philistines. Saul then will despair of searching for me anymore in all the territory of Israel, and I will escape from his hand' " (27:1).

David, in his great fear of what his unpredictable father-in-law could do to him, had apparently forgotten that he was the anointed of God. In one sense, this seems a strange turn of events for a man who had just witnessed to Saul, Abner, and all the soldiers on both sides. But we have to remember that although David was the anointed of God, so was Saul.

And with David's persistent refusal to harm Saul in any way, or to gain the kingdom for himself, he was left little choice but to keep on running.

This is not an attempt to excuse David's action but to help us understand what was going on inside of him. The depression he experienced was not simply an emotional low. It became a way of life for 16 months.

David took his wives, his 600 men and their households, and traveled to the land of the Philistines to dwell with Achish at Gath. Achish was the king before whom David had feigned insanity in order to escape. When Saul learned that David was in Gath, he sought him no more. David was at least right on that score.

When David requested a place where he and his men could live, Achish generously gave him Ziklag, where David remained for 16 months.

If you voluntarily go into the land of the Philistines, Satan will move in the hearts of your enemies to help you stay there as effortlessly as possible. Though Saul was the anointed of God, he certainly was out of the will of God in pursuing David; but he would gladly leave David alone in the land of the Philistines. King

Achish was generous and kind toward David during his stay in Gath. Satan is alive and well on planet Earth. If you drift out of the will of God, Satan will be delighted to make you comfortable.

In addition, if you drift out of the will of God, you may take your family with you, as well as other people who are closely associated with you. David's wives and 600 households were affected by his actions. In times of personal discouragement, we must be aware of our responsibility to other members of our family, as well as to other believers, and to business associates and neighbors.

During the 16 months, David developed a pattern of raiding the Geshurites and the Girzites and the Amalekites who had inhabited the land from ancient times. "And David attacked the land and did not leave a man or a woman alive, and he took away the sheep, the cattle, the donkeys, the camels, and the clothing. Then he returned and came to Achish" (27:9).

Although we might explain David's plundering and murdering by saying that he was providing for his family and friends, this certainly does not justify his actions. Many of us have large households, but we are never justified in breaking the law of God in order to meet these responsibilities.

When King Achish would ask David where he had raided on any particular day, David would lie and tell him that he was raiding in the south of Judah, naming one of several areas. Since David didn't leave anyone alive in the places he plundered, there was no one who could reveal exactly what he was doing.

Achish believed David's word, and thought that his behavior would make him so detestable to the people of Israel that David would be his servant as long as he lived.

It is important for us to remember that David was in the land of the enemy of his own free will. Contrast this to Paul being sent by God to a jail in Rome. Under these circumstances, Paul won a host of Roman soldiers into the family of God. During his time in jail, he sang hymns and rejoiced, and wrote letters to encourage Christians.

If you find yourself in the land of the enemy, evaluate why

you are there and whether your way of life is what it should be. If you are there in the will of God, you will have a song of peace in your heart, as Paul did, and you will be an encouragement and witness to others.

Get Ready for the War

About this time the Philistines began preparations for a war against Israel. "And Achish said to David, 'Know assuredly that you will go out with me in the camp, you and your men.' And David said to Achish, 'Very well, you shall know what your servant can do.' So Achish said to David, 'Very well, I will make you my bodyguard for life' " (28:1-2).

Meanwhile, back in Israel, when Saul realized that the Philistines were preparing for war, he was very troubled. He needed some guidance, but Samuel was dead.

Saul gathered his army together in Gilboa, and when he saw the camp of the Philistines, "he was afraid and his heart trembled greatly." When Saul inquired of the Lord, the Lord did not answer him, either by dreams or by Urim or by prophets. The Urim and Thummin were the special means of guidance associated with the ephod of the priest. Apparently, God had had enough of Saul and his disobedience, and would not respond to his inquiries and pleas. God "will not always strive with us; nor will He keep His anger forever" (Ps. 103:9).

Saul and the Witch

It didn't take Saul long to make another error. He asked his servants to find a woman who was a medium that he might ask her for guidance. The servants found a woman in Endor; and disguising himself, Saul went at night with two other men to talk with the witch. He was fully aware of the evilness of witchcraft, for he had already ordered such people out of the land. When Samuel had informed Saul that he was being rejected as king, he had told the king that his rebellion was "as the sin of divination" (1 Sam. 15:23). This sin had long been condemned among the people of Israel and was punishable by death. (See Ex. 22:18; Lev. 20:27; Deut. 18:10-14.)

When Saul asked the medium to bring up from the dead the person he would name, her response was, "Behold, you know what Saul has done, how he was cut off those who are mediums and spiritists from the land. Why are you then laying a snare for my life to bring about my death?" (1 Sam. 28:9) Saul vowed that she would not be punished for what she would do.

He asked the witch to bring up Samuel for him. She did so and then "cried out with a loud voice . . . 'Why have you deceived me? For you are Saul' " (28:12).

He asked her not to be afraid but to tell him what she was seeing. She described it as a divine being coming up, then as an old man wrapped with a robe.

By now Saul knew with certainty that it was Samuel, and he bowed with his face to the ground, in order to pay homage to the prophet. He then asked Samuel what he should do about the battle with the Philistines. Samuel replied, "Why then do you ask me, since the Lord has departed from you and has become your adversary?" Samuel went on to say that David would become king; he reminded Saul of his sin about the Amalekites, and promised that the next day Saul and his sons would be dead (28:16-19).

Saul hadn't eaten all day, and at the prediction of his death he collapsed in fear and weakness. The witch, who had every reason to be furious with Saul, showed consideration in asking the men to stay until she could prepare food for them.

Though I don't understand all the implications of this unusual story, there are things about it we can say for certain. It is obvious that Samuel did appear. There clearly is such a thing as the occult. The prophecies of Samuel did come to pass, prophecies which were fully recognizable to Saul as the word of Samuel and of the Lord.

Many people today read horoscopes daily to seek guidance for their lives. Ouija boards, tarot cards, the I Ching, séances, and forms of black magic are all common in North America. We are being warned in this story, as well as in other parts of the Word of God, that Christians are not to become involved with the occult.

We don't want to overlook the kindness shown by the witch of Endor. People who are involved in the occult often have fascinating personalities. They may be creative and witty, and give the impression that they have sincere compassion for others. But being nice does not necessarily make these people teachers of truth.

The Apostle John warned the Christians of the early church: "Beloved, do not believe every spirit, but test the spirits to see whether they are from God; because many false prophets have gone out into the world" (1 John 4:1). A practice such as sorcery, which is clearly in opposition to the Word of God, cannot be appropriate for a Christian.

David and the Philistines

Meanwhile, back in the Philistines' camp, David and his men were marching to war with Achish, much to the surprise of the Philistine princes. When they protested the presence of the Israelites, Achish defended David's loyalty. The princes didn't care how loyal David was; they didn't want him in their army because he was a traitor to his own people. "Make the man go back, that he may return to his place where you have assigned him, and do not let him go down to battle with us, lest in the battle he become an adversary to us. For with what could this man make himself acceptable to his lord? Would it not be with the heads of these men?" (1 Sam. 29:4)

King Achish went back and talked to David, conveying the message of the Philistine princes. Although David reaffirmed his loyalty, the princes had left no leeway, and Achish asked David and all his men to leave the following morning.

It is hard to believe that David could have been so totally confused and out of the will of God. Yet experience does show that many men and women of God have become depressed and discouraged, to the point where their Christian ministry and witness are totally lost through their own poor judgment. But God would not permit His chosen king to do this. Through the princes of the Philistines, God forced David out of his position of compromise.

Desolation at Ziklag

God sent further circumstances into David's life to bring him back to his senses. The Amalekites had invaded Ziklag and burned it and carried off the families of the 600 men. When David and his men returned to Ziklag, they were met by a scene of desolation, and assumed that their families had been killed. After all, when they raided, they didn't leave any survivors, so why would they expect anything different from their enemies? "David and the people who were with him lifted their voices and wept until there was no strength in them to weep" (30:4). After the men couldn't weep anymore, they became angry and talked of stoning David.

This whole series of tragic circumstances finally brought David to his senses, and he "strengthened himself in the Lord his God" (v. 6). Then he asked Abiathar to bring him the ephod, and David inquired of the Lord as to whether they should pursue the soldiers who had burned and robbed their city. God answered, "Pursue, for you shall surely overtake them, and you shall surely rescue all" (v. 8).

We need to learn from the volcanic life of David. God will permit us to drift out of His will into the land of the enemy. He will permit us to even break His laws, hoping that this will bring us to our senses. But thanks be to God, He is faithful to us, and will send circumstances into our lives until we finally are brought to our knees. God always forgives penitent sinners.

As David traveled with his 600 men toward the brook of Besor, 200 of them became too faint to go further in pursuit. So David left them with the baggage and went on with 400.

They came upon an Egyptian who was exhausted and hungry. After they had refreshed him with food and water, he informed them of the raid on Ziklag. He then showed them the way to where the Amalekites were eating, drinking, dancing, and celebrating the great spoil they had taken. David and his men attacked and won a complete victory. They rescued their wives and children, and took the spoils—their own goods and what had been taken from the Philistines—back to the brook of Besor.

David, who had been out of the will of God, was brought to his knees through sorrow so great that he wept until he could weep no more. Then he encouraged himself in God, turning to a faithful priest who brought the ephod. David cried out to God, who answered and led him through circumstances in which he recovered his family and the families of all his men, and doubled the spoils.

Why did God respond to David and not to Saul under similar circumstances? As an earthly father, can you imagine your son—a strong, valiant man of war—weeping until he could weep no more? How could God turn His back upon a penitent son like David? Saul was not penitent, and God did not answer him.

God touched David's heart through his family. This is a common soft spot in the hearts of many mighty men. God will use any means necessary to bring a compromised believer to his knees in penitence. He will lead that one through whatever circumstances are needed to accomplish His will.

What about the Spoils?

As the 400 soldiers with David came closer to the brook of Besor, a few of them must have eyed the amount of the spoils. They figured out how much they would get if it were divided 400 ways instead of 600. That answer was so much better that they decided the 200 who had stayed by the brook really didn't deserve a share.

Not only were the 200 men too faint to go to battle, but the entire army was a rather motley crew of discontents, debtors, and those in distress. We have to realize that God has chosen the foolish things to confound the wise. Not many mighty and noble are called. The church of God is filled with people who are not all outstanding citizens. Many are not strong enough to stand in the front line of the battle. It is sad to see some Christian leaders continually looking for only the beautiful and super-talented people to serve in their churches. God more often calls ordinary people into His service.

David was aware of this principle and responded: "You must not do so, my brothers, with what the Lord has given us, who has kept us and delivered into our hand the band that came against us. And who will listen to you in this matter? For as his share is who goes down to the battle, so shall his share be who stays by the baggage; they shall share alike" (30:23-24).

David realized that the spoil had actually been provided to them by God. From a practical point of view, all of us need to realize that though we work and plan diligently, our income and savings actually are provided by God, and belong to God.

The old story about the farmer is not far from the truth. As he watched one of his barns burning, he said, "Lord, *Your* barn is burning." Of course, the barns that were still standing belonged to God too. It is well for us to realize that everything we have belongs to God. We are sojourners on this earth, simply leasing what we think we own. We must learn to possess our possessions, and not be possessed *by* them. Many people have not learned this lesson.

Sharing Modern-Day Spoils

When we were in Africa, I found it heartwarming to see that every missionary received a set monthly allotment according to need and not according to the status of his job. Each adult missionary received the same amount, and families were given a sum for each child, depending on age.

My bride and I have tithed for more than 25 years. Our tithe to God is 10 percent of our income before taxes. This money is God's tithe, not our offering. However, to give tithes and offerings, a person has to learn to give and to save. And he must find a lifestyle that is compatible with God's purposes.

While struggling through medical school, Janet and I lived on a very meager income. Our tithe amounted to a widow's mite. A Christian physician told me at that time that the greatest pleasure he got out of his income was writing his tithe and offering checks each month. At that time, I thought he had flipped his lid, but as I have gotten older, I understand what he meant. It *is* more blessed to give than to receive. We must give, not of necessity, but because God loves a cheerful giver. We cannot out-give God.

If I offered you $100 but asked for $10 back, would you accept? How about $1,000 with $100 back? Or $10,000 with $1,000 returned? Everyone would say, "Yes, yes."

But when it comes to tithing—and as the tithe becomes bigger and bigger—instead of being overwhelmed by the generosity of God, we start looking at the purchasing power of the tithe. We think, *If I didn't give away so much, I could buy another condominium.* How many condominiums can you live in? How many cars can you drive? How many clothes can you wear? Most of us have so many clothes in our closets that the rods are almost falling off the walls.

There is real need for Christians to make a covenant with God about their tithes and offerings, and then to realize that it truly is a covenant which is to be kept. This is the only way my wife and I have been able to persistently continue tithing and giving offerings, year by year, as our income has increased. Otherwise, the purchasing power of the tithe would become an insurmountable barrier.

What does tithing do for people? It gives them a joy and a spirit of generosity that is very gratifying. It gives them an understanding of priorities in life. It helps them to organize their finances and live with what is left. Tithing does not necessarily lead to increased income, but it does lead to a sense of prosperity that passes understanding.

Wise Giving

After sharing the spoils with his 600 men, David sent gifts to people in many places in Israel, where he and his men had stayed during the years they had been fugitives. This shows David's sensitivity to those who had helped him and suggests that we should also give offerings to the places and people who have become part of our lives. I don't believe God expects us to give carelessly to organizations or individuals just because they make requests. We are to use discernment and good judgment about our giving.

I personally have found great joy in supporting organizations and people with whom I am involved. Many years ago, I became aware of responsible giving when I began to feel that we were writing some of our checks rather carelessly. The Lord and I had to have a discussion about this. I reminded Him about my grandmother, Mary Murray, who came from Glasgow, and that her Scottish blood runs in my veins. And then I said to the Lord, "I am willing to pay our tithe cheerfully, even hilariously, if You will show us very clearly that the need is there." I can assure you that from that day to this, there has never been a careless check given from the Jorden household. The needs have been very clearly pointed out by God, and in such number that we can hardly meet all the needs that we are aware of.

I have also learned that our gifts are a "sweet savor unto God." The results of my gifts are not my responsibility. David gave his presents without any strings attached, and you and I should also. We should not attempt to control the organizations or people to whom we give our tithes and offerings. They are sweet savors unto God, and if we give them in secret, God will reward us openly.

No one should tell you where to give your tithes and offerings. But your local church, where you and your family worship, should share a portion. God will also lay on your heart certain needs that He wants you to meet. Some may be close at hand. Remember the story about poor Lazarus who lay at the rich man's door day after day? The rich man had walked over Lazarus for months or years and had never met his need. You and I can have people nearby who need provisions, while we are ignorant of their needs, or calloused to them. If we ask God, He will show us the needs.

The Word of God has much to say about giving, and makes it clear that we are to give our time, talents, and our whole selves to God, as well as our money. As Peter said to the crippled man, "I do not possess silver and gold, but what I do have I give to you: In the name of Jesus Christ the Nazarene—walk!" (Acts 3:6)

Let me give you some other references which speak about giving. You can look them up at your convenience if you are interested: Joshua 1:6-9; Proverbs 3:9-10; 11:24-25; Malachi 3:6-12; Luke 6:38; Acts 20:33-35; 2 Corinthians 9:5-15; Ephesians 4:28.

Giving of Yourself
As a doctor, I am reminded of the need to give of myself. On Sunday mornings, I make hospital rounds and tend to hurry a bit

so that I will be on time to church. But one Sunday morning it seemed that every patient I saw had a list of questions a mile long. It was really important for me to arrive at church on time that day—just like the Levite and priest who walked by the wounded man. They were on their way to a Deeper Life Seminar and they were in a rush.

Well, that particular morning I was trying desperately to get out of the hospital when the Lord spoke to me, "Paul, reach out and touch these people today. They need you."

I slowed my pace and tried to meet their needs. Yes, I came strolling into church rather late, but somehow there was a warm feeling that I was doing what God intended me to do. If I don't have time to meet the needs of people in the hospital who are under my care, what is life all about? If you don't have interest and compassion to meet the needs of people in your care, what is your life all about?

Begin right in your own home. If you don't have time for your spouse and children, what is the meaning of your life? That is where you live. We all face the dilemma of demands on our time, and I certainly don't have all the answers. But I do know that we are to be hilarious givers, not only of our money, but of ourselves and our time. If we do this, God will bless us deep inside. From the world's point of view, this is a strange philosophy, but it is based on the reality of God Himself.

The Death of Saul

While David was beginning to taste the joy of victory, Saul and his army were tasting the agony of defeat. They had fought against the Philistines and had fled. Saul's three sons had been killed, and Saul himself was badly wounded. However, he was conscious and rational, and asked his armor bearer, "Draw your sword and pierce me through with it, lest these uncircumcised come and pierce me through and make sport of me" (1 Sam. 31:4).

Though Saul had in many ways been a good man, he had never really recognized that God was in control of his life. He had been disobedient to God repeatedly. Now that he was mortally wounded, there was no evidence that he turned his mind and heart toward Almighty God. Rather, he continued to think of what men might do to him.

As a physician I often see people who are very aware that they are near death. And I am astonished how many of them have no spiritual insight at all, no recognition of God.

Saul showed no fear of death, for he asked his armor bearer to kill him. However, the young man was afraid to do so. And so the King took his own sword and fell upon it. When the armor bearer saw that Saul was dead, he likewise took his own sword and died with his king.

Suicide

Suicide is a very troublesome problem for those who survive the one who has died. We are bothered by the possibility that the person may have gone insane. We can accept heart attacks, gall bladder attacks, or accidents, but we have difficulty with mental illness. Yet God has made us with mind, body, and soul. We fear that perhaps a believer has gone to hell for committing suicide.

Although Saul had been badly wounded, I still consider that he committed suicide and I don't think that he went to hell because of it. I believe he will be in heaven. He certainly is not going to have a front row seat, but I think he will be there. He was the chosen and anointed of God. Saul broke several of the Ten Commandments, but he did not, as far as we know, commit the unforgiveable sin of blasphemy against the Holy Spirit.

The person who commits suicide causes great grief to many people. His loved ones not only grieve the loss of a dear one, but often wonder whether they caused the suicide or could have prevented it.

In my opinion, suicide is not a Christian option. However, I enlarge the definition of suicide to much more than is commonly meant by that word. Suicide is thought about and contemplated far more than is generally known. Some people lead to their own deaths by ignoring serious physical symptoms, when they should get immediate medical attention. Others hasten death by reckless driving. What looks like an accident is often a case of suicide.

Many people dull their senses with drugs and alcohol to the point that they are not thinking clearly and then commit suicide. By drugs I am not referring primarily to illegal forms, but to those which can be obtained by prescription or over the counter. Such individuals are placing a much lower value on human life than God places on it. They are not behaving as people who know they have been created in the image of God. It may well be that our churches need to do more to *stress the value of the person* in the eyes of God, and *demonstrate the value of the person* within the church.

After Saul's Death

As a result of this battle, the people of Israel not only lost their king, but also lost their cities, for the Philistines came to dwell in them. On the next day, when the Philistines came to strip the slain, they found Saul and his three sons on Mount Gilboa. "And they cut off his head, and stripped off his weapons, and sent them throughout the land of the Philistines, to carry the good news to the house of their idols and to the people. And they put his weapons in the temple of Ashtaroth, and they fastened his body to the wall of Bethshan" (31:9-10).

One group of people was extremely loyal to Saul. The valiant men of Jabesh-gilead walked all night to retrieve the bodies of Saul and his sons. They took the bodies back to Jabesh, burned them, buried the bones, and then fasted for seven days. To fully understand the loyalty of the people of Jabesh-gilead, you will need to read two other stories in the Bible, found in 1 Samuel 11 and Judges 19. Saul was a relative to these people, and they were not going to leave their kinsman without a decent burial.

מָגֵן דָּוִד

6
Waiting Upon the Lord

2 SAMUEL 1—4

God continued preparing David to reign as the second king of Israel by allowing him to wait. This is a hard lesson for all of us to learn, and it was especially difficult for a man like David.

There is a balance in the Christian life between waiting on the Lord and actively responding to opportunities in God's plan for us. We need to be finely tuned to both the waiting and the going ahead, so that we will know what is God's will for any given time.

David began now to move into a time which combined waiting and increased decision-making. As we respond to opportunities to serve God, some of the decisions we make are good, some not so good, and others downright bad. However, God does not expect us to be perfect, but to be obedient and open to learning His ways.

We see David as he began to assume responsibilities and to make necessary decisions. Some of them were difficult for him and we could speculate as to whether they were good or bad decisions, but that is not really important. As he made decisions, he was being prepared, step by step, to serve as the second king of Israel.

Saul's Death Reported

The Book of 2 Samuel is a continuation of the life of David and might be considered as part of 1 Samuel. The scene shifts from Saul to David, as the report of Saul's death arrives. There has been much disagreement about which story of Saul's death is correct. Did Saul die by himself, or did the Amalekite finish him off? I don't see much significance in the disagreement. The young man who comes to our attention in 2 Samuel 1 was probably with Saul when he died, because he brought the crown and bracelet from the dead king. He had no scruples against helping the anointed of the Lord to his death. He was merely performing an act of mercy. I assume that he was telling the truth, and that his presence was not reported in 1 Samuel 31. However, in the repetition of the story, we are reminded that Saul decided to end his own life, one way or another, and that is not an option for an obedient Christian.

David had returned to Ziklag, after recovering the women and children, and had remained in the destroyed city for two days waiting for word. On the third day, when a young man arrived who had been in Saul's camp, David was eager for news.

When the young man reported the deaths of Saul and Jonathan, David asked him how he knew they were dead. The man told the following story:

By chance I happened to be on Mount Gilboa, and behold, Saul was leaning on his spear. And behold, the chariots and the horsemen pursued him closely. And when he looked behind him, he saw me, and called to me. And I said, "Here I am."

And he said to me, "Who are you?"

And I answered him, "I am an Amalekite."

Then he said to me, "Please stand beside me and kill me; for agony has seized me because my life still lingers in me."

So I stood beside him and killed him, because I knew that he could not live after he had fallen. And I took the crown which was on his head and the bracelet which was on his arm, and I have brought them here to my lord (1:6-10).

Some have suggested that the Amalekite really performed a mercy killing. And that brings the story right into our own time. As a physician, I am very aware of mercy killing or euthanasia, and am very opposed to it. It is one thing to let a patient die a normal death with dignity; it is quite another thing to terminate that life deliberately. The physician must realize that he is not God. It is not for him to determine when a person's life will come to a close or when the patient has suffered enough.

My job as a physician is to keep the patient comfortable, and to do what I can, within reason, to keep him alive. Though quality of life is more important than quantity of life, it is for God to decide when a life will end.

Many people feel that a physician has some magic by which to end a life. The decision to terminate life does not belong to any individual. If someone is going to end another's life, what is the difference if it is done by a massive use of drugs, by a plastic bag over the head, by a bullet, or by injecting air into the veins?

David's Reaction

When David heard of Saul's death, he and all the men with him tore their clothes, and mourned and wept and fasted until evening: Their grief was for Saul and Jonathan, as well as for the people of Israel who had fallen before the Philistines.

During these hours of grief, David made a decision—one that causes me some difficulty. He called the young man to him, asked where he was from, and then said, "How is it you were not afraid to stretch out your hand to destroy the Lord's anointed?" (1:14)

Then David called one of his men and told him to kill the Amalekite. David said to the offender, "Your blood is on your head, for your mouth has testified against you saying, 'I have killed the Lord's anointed'" (1:16).

It seems to me that David was applying the standards of the people of God to this Amalekite. But the Law was given to the people of God, not to the heathen. David was requiring spiritual standards of a nonbeliever. However, it was not a snap decision nor was it made in anger. The decision stood and the young Amalekite died.

Lament for Jonathan and Saul

The last nine verses of 2 Samuel 1 are David's lamentation for Saul and Jonathan. He called them "beloved and pleasant in their life." Saul—beloved and pleasant? Was David going through a customary eulogy, being gracious to a king who had passed on? I don't think so. We all have had relationships that have soured, but about which we can remember very happy times from earlier days. Saul had been David's father-in-law, and father of his dear friend Jonathan.

David said about Jonathan, "Your love to me was more wonderful than the love of women." What was he saying? Was this a deviate relationship, as some people have tried to suggest? No, it wasn't. David was saying exactly what he meant. The love he and Jonathan had for each other was one of total commitment. But can two men deeply love one another? Absolutely.

In one hospital where I was on the staff, two of the doctors had known each other since early childhood. After 30 years of close friendship, they even looked alike. It was a pleasant thing to see the love these two men had for each other, a love which did not in any way interfere with their love for their wives and children.

In our day of blatant openness about homosexuality, we need to be careful not to rob genuine friendships of their strength and goodness by suggesting that there is anything wrong in them. Men need one another's friendship and the commitment of true love. But in no way does this include a sexual relationship.

On to Hebron

David went to the Lord to inquire, "Shall I go up to one of the cities of Judah?" (2:1) You see, David was still in the land of the Philistines. Though he was getting right with his God, he was still in the wrong place geographically. The Lord told him to go.

David became more specific now. "Where shall I go?" And God said, "To Hebron."

In this I see a lesson about the way God leads us. He never sends us off into confusion. A prospective missionary might say, "I'll go anywhere." But sooner or later, he has to buy a plane ticket to a specific place. In his praying, David followed the sense of direction that he had, and God guided him from there.

David and all his men and their families traveled to Hebron. I like this reference to the families. These men had been off to war, living in unpleasant surroundings; but their families had been near them. Now they all went together to Hebron.

I am concerned about men who feel that God's leading is consistently separating them from their families. I personally am sensitive to this, because I constantly make decisions in my own life about what I can and can't do. A conscious effort must be made to keep the family together as a unit, just as much as possible. I don't believe God wants families divided for long periods of time. There are exceptions, of course, but it seems to me that Christian men need to be more aware of their responsibility to maintain the unity of their families.

There are still situations where the children of missionaries are away from their parents for months at a time, in boarding schools. Couples must examine their hearts before the Lord, to see why they are putting their children in boarding school. Is this truly God's will for both parents and children? I have seen a few cases that made me wonder if missionary parents just wanted to be free of the responsibility of rearing their children. Missionaries need to carefully examine their priorities in life before the Lord; they need to be very sure that their children truly are supposed to go through these long separations from their parents.

King over Judah

The men of Judah came and anointed David king over the house of Judah. Now this was only 1 of the 12 tribes of Israel, but David had waited patiently and long for even this part of his coronation.

After Saul's death, a mighty man of valor might well have moved quickly, taking the kingdom by force. But this was not David's nature.

David's first recorded act as king was to send word to the men of Jabesh-gilead, thanking them for burying Saul and his sons. Then he added, "And now may the Lord show loving-kindness and truth to you; and I also will show this goodness to you, because you have done this thing. Now therefore, let your hands be strong, and be valiant; for Saul your lord is dead, and also the house of Judah has anointed me king over them" (2:6-7).

To some of the people of Jabesh-gilead, this would have brought back memories of the distant time in which their kinship with Saul had been formed. In that day, Judah had been the first tribe to act. (See Jud. 19—21; 21:18.)

Also, David was gently telling the loyalists of Saul that one of the tribes of Israel had already selected him as leader.

The Two Generals
Abner, Saul's commanding general, was the son of Ner, who was a brother to Saul's father, Kish. Throughout Saul's reign, there was a close personal relationship between these first cousins. A few years after Saul's death, Abner proclaimed the one remaining son, Ishbosheth, as king of Israel, but maintained control of the kingdom himself. During the seven and one-half years from the death of Saul to the joining of the kingdom, the forces of David and Ishbosheth were meeting in combat with some regularity. Because Abner was cousin to Saul, he was second cousin to Michal and therefore also to David by marriage.

Joab, David's commanding general, is first introduced to us here. His mother was David's sister Zeruiah, and his brothers were Asahel and Abishai. These three young men were wild ones and David had difficulty controlling them, especially Joab.

Waiting with Confidence
By the time Abner appointed Ishbosheth king, David had already waited for several years to be king of the whole nation, in addition to the 10—12 years before he became king of Judah.

Our lives are so often affected by other people. We may feel that God is leading in a certain direction, and we have a job to do for Him. Then all of a sudden, someone else takes over in an area we were heading for, and really causes us problems. We can do one of two things: either recognize that God is in control, or take matters into our own hands.

If you find yourself in a position of waiting for God to bring you to the time and place of His choosing, I hope you can know the confidence that David seemed to have. God will guide you, and you will gain strength in waiting upon Him.

Some people suffer fatigue that is largely emotional, from boredom, impatience, lack of peace, nervousness, or guilt. God does not intend His children to live this way. He wants us to wait upon Him with confidence that He will do things in His way and in His time. "Those who wait for the Lord will gain new strength; they will mount up with wings like eagles, they will run and not get tired, they will walk and not become weary" (Isa. 40:31).

I wonder if David wrote Psalm 37 during these years of waiting. Three times in the psalm, he said, "Fret not yourself." I don't know anything more needed by Christians today than a trust in God that chooses to: do good, cultivate faithfulness, commit one's way to God, rest in Him, wait patiently for Him, cease from anger, and forsake wrath. I hope you will read this wonderful psalm if you are in a time of waiting upon God.

Slaughter at the Pool

One day when Abner and his men went to Gibeon, they met up with Joab and his soldiers by the pool of Gibeon. The two groups sat down on either side of the pool. Abner suggested to Joab that the young soldiers have a contest to pass the time, and Joab agreed. Twelve men from each side were picked, and they stood in two rows. Each soldier reached over to his opponent, grabbed him by the head, and thrust a sword into him. All 24 men were soon dead. This was the start of a severe battle between the two sides, in which Joab's men gained the advantage and defeated the men of Israel.

Joab's brothers were in the battle, and one of them, Asahel, decided to chase after Abner. He is described as being "swift-footed as one of the gazelles which is in the field" (2 Sam. 2:18). He was part of the winning army and wanted some spoils from the battle.

Abner kept on running, but looked back now and then to try to dissuade Asahel from following him. Abner suggested he pursue one of the younger men and get the spoils from him. But Asahel would not listen. Then Abner said, "Turn aside from following me. Why should I strike you to the ground? How then could I lift up my face to your brother Joab?" (2:22)

However, Asahel refused to listen and Abner "struck him in the belly with the butt end of the spear, so that the spear came out at his back. And he fell there and died on the spot" (v. 23).

Asahel's brothers, Joab and Abishai, continued to pursue Abner until sundown. Then the sons of Benjamin stood behind Abner on a hill, as he called to Joab to ask, "Shall the sword devour forever? Do you not know that it will be bitter in the end? How long will you refrain from telling the people to turn back from following their brothers?" (2:26)

This seemed to make sense to Joab; he blew his trumpet to halt the people and stop the fighting. When the generals took the toll of the battle, they found 20 dead for Joab and 360 dead for Abner.

Ishbosheth and Abner

The skirmishes went on between the forces of Abner and Joab, and the house of Saul grew weaker as the house of David grew stronger. Not only was David's army gaining, but so was his own household, as he produced six sons from six different wives.

Circumstances can be used as part of the plan of God. As the war continued between the house of David and the house of Saul, Abner became increasingly powerful. Then Ishbosheth, king of Israel, accused his older cousin Abner of consorting with Saul's concubine Rizpah. This was a very serious accusation, for it was the exclusive right of a successor to a king to cohabit with the concubines of the deceased ruler. If Abner were truly ruling, as some people believe, he may have felt he had the right to take

Rizpah into his harem. Or he may not have gone near her. In any event, the challenge of Ishbosheth sent him into a rage:

Am I a dog's head that belongs to Judah? Today I show kindness to the house of Saul your father, and to his brothers and to his friends, and have not delivered you into the hands of David; and today you charge me with a guilt concerning the woman. May God do so to Abner, and more also, if as the Lord has sworn to David, I do not accomplish this for him, to transfer the kingdom from the house of Saul, and to establish the throne of David over Israel and over Judah, from Dan even to Beersheba (3:8-10).

Abner promptly sent messengers to David, offering to bring all of Israel into the kingdom of David, if David would make a league with him. David replied with positive interest, but stated one condition for a covenant between them—he wanted Michal back.

David and Michal

David's request was a strange one because he already had multiple wives. We might think that David was romantically desiring the return of his first wife, but there is no evidence that he inquired of her well-being or happiness. We know that Michal loved David before she married him, but we have no indication that David needed Michal at this time in his life. He had more than an adequate number of wives to satisfy his sexual needs.

I believe he wanted Michal either out of lust or to satisfy his male ego. This would also reinstate him as the king's son-in-law, and strengthen his claim to the throne.

When David's men went to retrieve Michal, Abner traveled with them to make sure she cooperated. Her husband Paltiel, who loved her very much, walked along behind the soldiers and Michal, weeping in terrible grief. Abner watched him for a while, and then bluntly told him to go home. She had to be returned to David.

In my opinion, the two greatest potential problems in marriage are sex and money (or property). Money is often related to power. In the return of Michal, I think we are seeing a combination of the two. She represented property because she had been David's wife. From a political point of view, Michal was the daughter of the king. Also, through her would be some succession to the throne. Some scholars wonder if certain inheritance rights in Israel passed through the woman at this time.

David lived in a day when polygamy was acceptable. At least there is no condemnation of it in the Old Testament. I think that today's men can understand this story of David better than the ladies can, since most women tend to be monogamist in their attitudes, while the average male is a polygamist at heart.

As it turned out, David didn't appear to have gained any advantage from having Michal back. Nor did he seem attached to her emotionally. So I would conclude that one of his reasons for wanting her back was lust, or sex without love. Most women know that sex without love is not very satisfying. We men haven't learned the lesson as well, but we have only been around for 6,000 years. So hang in there, ladies—maybe there is still hope for us.

We live in a day of great tolerance for sex without marriage, for children born out of wedlock, for extramarital affairs, and for divorce on flimsy grounds. All of these tolerant attitudes *do* influence people, and the problem of lust is one that every person has to face. Not only do we have our own sexual drives to contend with, but we are bombarded daily by suggestive stories and commercials from both television and magazines.

What is lust? It is not just looking. We men enjoy the feminine scenery, but we should know when enjoyment turns to lustful fantasies. If we don't stop right there, we are heading for trouble.

Being a Christian should make a real difference in a man's relationships with women. He should be able to enjoy knowing them as friends, and not continually be tormented by lustful thoughts. This type of friendship is possible if a man's commitment to his wife is second only to his love and commitment to God.

Another aspect I want to mention here is that sex carries with it responsibility. We need to emphasize this to our young people, impressing them with the fact that if they parent a child, they are legally responsible until that child has finished his schooling. We must inform our children that God doesn't intend sex to be an isolated emotional high, as it is frequently portrayed in movies and television. People who are mature physically can produce babies. But it takes parents who are mature in their minds and spirits to raise children well.

On this point of responsibility, I return to David. I feel that David didn't realize his responsibility to Michal when he decided to get her back. I don't think he considered Michal's welfare or her feelings for her husband, Paltiel. He simply used his power and said, "I want her back."

Transfer of Power

After Michal arrived in Hebron, Abner consulted with the elders of Israel. We can see the influence and strength this man held in the nation. When he said, "It is time to transfer loyalty to David," they did so.

Abner brought 20 men with him to Hebron, and David had a feast prepared for them. One of David's stronger characteristics, as we saw in his relationship with Saul, was that he did not hold vengeance in his heart. David could have felt anger toward Abner for his opposition all these years. After all, Abner had been the primary person standing between David and the throne of Israel, from the time of Saul's death until now.

However, David also knew that Abner was the one man who could bring the nation to him. This was the way God's purpose would be accomplished.

After the feast Abner said to David, "Let me arise and go, and gather all Israel to my lord the king that they may make a covenant with you, and that you may be king over all that your soul desires" (3:21).

At the same time David was sending Abner away in peace, Joab and his soldiers were returning with a great spoil from the Philistines. Joab was immediately informed that Abner had come to David, and had left in peace.

Joab faced this situation with intensity, as he challenged David: "What have you done? . . . You know Abner the son of Ner, that he came to deceive you and learn of your going out and coming in, and to find out all that you are doing" (3:24-25). Joab then left David and sent messengers to bring Abner back.

The Death of Abner

"When Abner returned to Hebron, Joab took him aside into the middle of the gate to speak with him privately, and there he struck him in the belly, so that he died on account of the blood of Asahel his brother" (3:27). Joab had two good reasons, humanly speaking, for killing Abner. First, he was avenging the death of his brother; and second, he was making sure that he would not be replaced as commander of David's army. However, neither of these reasons justifies killing a man in cold blood. Yet how easy it is to explain away sin, either by saying it was for a good reason, or that the sin wasn't very serious.

When David heard of the murder, he made a public statement: "I and my kingdom are innocent before the Lord forever of the blood of Abner the son of Ner. May it fall on the head of Joab and on all his father's house; and may there not fail from the house of Joab one who has a discharge, or who is a leper, or who takes hold of a distaff, or who falls by the sword, or who lacks bread" (3:28-29).

David then ordered Joab and all the people to tear their clothes, wear sackcloth, and mourn before Abner's body. King David himself walked behind the bier as they went to bury Abner in Hebron. At the gravesite, the king lifted up his voice and wept, as did all the people. And then David chanted a lament for Abner: "Should Abner die as a fool dies? Your hands were not bound, nor your feet put in fetters; As one falls before the wicked, you have fallen" (3:33-34).

Throughout the day David continued to mourn and fast. When people tried to persuade him to eat, he refused, saying he would eat nothing until sundown. The people were very pleased by the public demonstration of sorrow, and understood clearly that Abner's death had not been David's desire. David was genuinely mourning Abner, as he had mourned Saul and Jonathan. He realized that these men had played a role in his life, within the purpose of Almighty God.

Of Abner David said, "Do you not know that a prince and a great man has fallen this day in Israel?" Of himself he said, "I am weak today, though anointed king." Of Joab and his brothers he said, "These men the sons of Zeruiah are too difficult for me. May the Lord repay the evildoer according to his evil" (3:38-39).

How do you respond to people who don't agree with you? To people who give you and your projects a hard time? Can you say, "He is a great guy—I just don't agree with his opinion on this matter"? When you serve on a board, are you able to be in the minority and think that the majority are fine people? Or do you wonder if they have their heads screwed on backwards because they don't agree with you? David had a tremendous ability to respect the people whom God brought into his life, even though they didn't always agree with him.

"They Are Too Much for Me"

As David admitted that he couldn't manage Joab and his brother, he gave the whole situation to the Lord. And as our children grow older, there are times that they are simply too strong-willed to control. In saying this, I am not excusing the father from his responsibility to manage his family. A child needs to be disciplined from the time he is young so that he will be manageable in his teen years. And yet, even when this seems to have been done, there are some young people who are very rebellious in their teenage years.

It is necessary to commit these mustangs to God, asking Him to tame them in His way. The prodigal son finally came to his senses, after going through famine, hunger, and the insult of working in a pig pen. He returned to his father's house and was reinstated in the family. In Joab's case, he served David during all his years as king.

I don't want to leave the impression that all you can do for your children is pray. God has put you parents in a position of leadership in your homes, and you should maintain as much control as possible. If your child presents you with a problem you can solve, then solve it. It isn't necessary to ask your son to pray with you about something you already know how to deal with. God isn't going to do your work in the family, but He'll guide you.

When your teenagers behave in a totally unacceptable way, it is proper to pray, and it is also proper to confront them and say,

"It just isn't going to be that way!" You are the adults. It is your home and you set the standards. You have every right to expect your children to live by your standards while you are supporting them. Just recently I heard of a young man who wanted to live in his parents' home with his girlfriend. He couldn't understand why his parents didn't like that idea. The father firmly said, "Not in my house."

As parents you are to shoulder your responsibility. You can't give it to God. You are to be leaders in your homes, not as dictators but as wise, responsible, and loving parents, training your children. Of course, there will be disagreements at times about nonessentials. But in issues where morality, or parent survival, or the future well-being of the child is involved, there can be no compromise.

Don't feel that you have to be perfect or know everything around your children. Don't be ashamed to tell your teenagers that you don't understand something. They don't expect you to be perfect or to know all things. They can relate better to vulnerable parents who are dependent upon God. This can result in positive lessons in faith.

Death of Ishbosheth and His Killers
Saul's son Ishbosheth was murdered in his bed by two men named Rechab and Baanah. They beheaded him, and brought the head to David, thinking that they had done him a favor. While David was unable to manage a man like Joab, he was certainly able to handle this. He reminded the two men that he had put to death the Amalekite who had killed Saul. "How much more, when wicked men have killed a righteous man in his own house on his bed, shall I not now require his blood from your hand, and destroy you from the earth?" (4:11)

David ordered his men to kill these two and to hang their hands and feet beside the pool in Hebron as a public warning.

Close to Coronation
God had been preparing David for his coronation day. David had accepted the responsibility of making decisions, and had recog-

nized that God was in control of all aspects of his life. He had learned much about waiting upon the Lord, and now, at last, the day was almost at hand when David would be king of all Israel.

מָגֵן דָּוִד

7
The Price of Success

2 SAMUEL 5—10

Every successful man knows there is a price to pay for success. This price may include personal effort, recognition, responsibility, temptation, battles, failure, frustration and persistence, marital tension, disappointment, prayer for the future, commitment, fame and generosity. Often a successful man—or woman—pays a price physically and emotionally, and the family is forced to share in paying that price.

As David came to the time of his coronation, he was 37 years old, but was probably considerably older than that in maturity. He had a lot of miles on him! His coronation occurred seven and one-half years after he began his reign over Judah. It might seem that this is a long time for a man like David to wait. But we must realize that he was not just sitting around waiting for the coronation to occur. A successful man is always busy with many activities. Usually he puts in long years of training before he receives his "coronation."

It is interesting to note that the elders came to David to anoint him. He did not seek them out, but they honored the agreement made with Abner. When they came to David at Hebron they said, "Behold, we are your bone and your flesh. Previously, when Saul was king over us, you were the one who led Israel out and in. And the Lord said to you, 'You will shepherd My people Israel, and you will be a ruler over Israel' " (5:1-2).

After all the elders had made a covenant with David, they anointed him to be king over Israel. In waiting for the elders to come to him, David demonstrated patience. Though it had taken a long time, David had waited for the appropriate timing to achieve his success. I see a lesson in this. Although a Christian man may pursue success in terms of competence and skill in his profession or trade, I don't feel it appropriate for him to seek money and prestige as primary goals of success. The man of God needs to realize that God is in control, and that his coronation will occur in God's way and in God's time. Making lots of money is not a proper goal for a Christian. In fact, the Apostle Paul warns that "he who would be rich brings many snares upon himself." (See 1 Tim. 6:9.)

Personal Effort

Not only is personal effort necessary to achieve success, but it is also needed to maintain the success.

David's first major action as king was to capture Jerusalem, taking it from the people of Jebus who were natives of the territory. Jerusalem was situated on a mountain, thus making it difficult to attack. Because of this, and because of its central location between northern and southern Israel, it was an ideal site for David's proposed capital.

Once before David had tried to replace his commander Joab with the general Abner. Now he tried again by saying that whoever entered the city of Jerusalem and struck down a Jebusite first would be chief and commander. Joab, being a competitive military man, saw to it that he was the first to enter. Some historians think that David's army entered the city through the water tunnel, a concealed passageway cut down through the rock under the city.

Recognition

Recognition of one's work is generally part of success. After gaining possession of the city, David quickly moved into the stronghold and called it "the city of David." Then he began building outward from Millo, one of his fortifications. During these years, "David became greater and greater, for the Lord God of hosts was with him" (2 Sam. 5:10).

To recognize David's growing prestige, and as an act of friendship, Hiram, king of Tyre, sent messengers to David. They came bearing cedar trees from which carpenters would construct a house for the king.

All of a sudden King David was an important man to his neighbors. Similar sudden recognition happens to people today. I was astonished, after obtaining my M.D. and license to practice medicine, to receive several requests for speaking engagements and committee assignments. Although I didn't feel any wiser for having received the degree, others recognized the increased wisdom of this brilliant young doctor!

Responsibility

Accompanying personal effort and recognition is the increased responsibility of being a successful person.

David quickly perceived the responsibility that was his as king of Israel, for he "realized that the Lord had established him as king over Israel, and that He had exalted his kingdom for the sake of His people Israel" (5:12). From that point forward, David would have to conduct himself not simply as a man, but as the king of Israel.

This reminds me of the public expectation that a doctor will have a certain manner about him, which includes dressing in a style which befits his profession. I must admit that I fail in this respect at times. I delight in dressing in my old clothes, especially when I am working around the house.

A few years ago, one of my daughters arrived home from school with a boy I hadn't met. As they came up the driveway, she saw me trimming the evergreens. I was in raggy old shorts and was sweating profusely. She waved cheerfully, walked over with her friend and said, "Kevin, this is our gardener, Paul." Kevin, not knowing the difference, shook hands with me, and I enjoyed going along with the joke.

Temptation

Added responsibility and influence bring added temptation, which often hits a man at his weakest spot. As success becomes greater, a man's dependence upon God must be strengthened in order for him to say "No" to the many temptations which will come his way.

During the early years of his reign in Jerusalem, David fathered 14 more children by his many wives, and others by his concubines. (See 1 Chron. 3:5-9.) While by custom David had a king's right to take wives and concubines, he was violating an explicit instruction found in Deuteronomy 17:17: "Neither shall he [the king] multiply wives for himself, lest his heart turn away; nor shall he greatly increase silver and gold for himself."

These two prohibited things—multiplied wives and multiplied gain—are the two greatest problems in our own society. We call them casual sex and greed for money. The modern practice of having one wife and one mistress usually ends up with one mistress after another. And they do not satisfy the male heart. As soon as the novelty wears off, the present one is replaced by another. Nor does money satisfy. One of the multimillionaires of the 20th century was asked how much money was enough. He answered, "Just a little more than I have."

Because a man on the way up, or a man at the top, is confronted with persuasive temptation, he needs firm guidelines. And these David had in the Word of God, as recorded in Deuteronomy 17:17. To show how a king was to resist these temptations, the passage continued: "Now it shall come about when he sits on the throne of his kingdom, he shall write for himself a copy of this

Law . . . and he shall read it all the days of his life, that he may learn to fear the Lord his God, by carefully observing all the words of this Law and these statutes, that his heart may not be lifted up above his countrymen and that he may not turn aside from the commandment" (vv. 18-20).

This strong emphasis upon the Word of God, not only reading it, but carefully observing it, is the key for successful and godly men, even in the last part of the 20th century.

I personally find direction in Jesus' teaching in the Sermon on the Mount. "Do not lay up for yourselves treasures upon earth, where moth and rust destroy, and where thieves break in and steal. But lay up for yourselves treasures in heaven, where neither moth nor rust destroys, and where thieves do not break in or steal" (Matt. 6:19-20). "You have heard that it was said, 'You shall not commit adultery'; but I say to you, that everyone who looks on a woman to lust for her has committed adultery with her already in his heart" (Matt. 5:27-28).

If you are obsessed with making money, or with seeking sexual gratification outside of marriage, I pray that the Spirit of God will warn you that these are not the true answers to your deepest needs.

Battles

When a man becomes powerful, he usually encounters a few people who try to strip him of part of his success. When the Philistines heard that David had become king of Israel, they prepared to attack him. The Philistines gathered in the Valley of Rephaim, which is near Jerusalem.

Though David had broken the biblical standards for a king, he was still conscious of God, and now asked for guidance as to whether he should fight the enemy. The Lord said to him, "Go up, for I will certainly give the Philistines into your hand" (2 Sam. 5:19). David was victorious in the battle and said, "The Lord has broken through my enemies before me like the breakthrough of waters" (v. 20).

A Christian today must remember that there will be attacks from the enemy. Satan is relentless in his warfare against Christians.

But as believers we have available a power much greater than any on earth.

Once again the Philistines attacked David and once again he went to God for guidance. How does a person receive direction from God?

Some years ago, when the office building I was renting went up for sale, I had to make a decision about whether or not to buy it. I already had a big mortgage on my house. With too many kids and too many expenses, I was dragging my feet about buying the building.

Finally, the owner of the building told me I would have to make a decision, because he had another potential buyer. I was awake all that night, not worrying, but in what I call "prayerful thought." And it was one of the few times in my life I had to say to God, "I cannot make this decision. You have to give me specific instructions as to what You want me to do." As a surgeon, I am almost ashamed of my inability to make a decision. After all, a surgeon may often be wrong, but he is never in doubt!

The very next morning the owner of the building *came to me* and said, "Paul, you will have to give me your decision. I have a buyer." He named the possible buyer, a man from whom I couldn't rent office space. I knew his priorities in life too well. Deep in my heart, I felt that this was very clear guidance from God, and so I bought the building. For a couple of years, that building was not exactly the greatest thing in my life. But as the years have passed, it has turned out to be the best financial investment that I have ever made.

God instructed David regarding this battle: "You shall not go directly up; circle around behind them and come at them in front of the balsam trees. And it shall be, when you hear the sound of marching in the tops of the balsam trees, then you shall act promptly, for then the Lord will have gone out before you to strike the army of the Philistines" (5:23-24).

David did exactly as God said, and chased and struck down the Philistines from Geba all the way to Gezer which was nearly back to their own land.

The balsam fir, to which God referred, was a tree from which balm was obtained, and was also called a "baka shrub." The balm was spoken of in a poetic and figurative way in the Scriptures, as well as being an object of trade at that time. These fir trees grew in the land of Gilead, near Gibeon where David was battling the Philistines.

In Psalm 84, the sons of Korah spoke of traveling through the Valley of Baca, or the balsams, on the way to Jerusalem. This place was called the Valley of Weeping because of the sound the trees made when the wind blew through them. However, in the psalm it also had a figurative meaning: a valley of weeping which the travelers would make into a place of springs. "The early rain also covers it with blessings. They go from strength to strength. Every one of them appears before God in Zion" (vv. 6-7).

In Isaiah 28:21, we find a reference to those two battles in a prophetic word from God: "For the Lord shall arise as on Mount Perazim, and be indignant as in the Valley of Gibeon, to do His work, His strange work, and to perform His task, His unusual task" (BERK.).

Failure

Successful people are well aware that they do not always succeed, that they sometimes fail. At times these failures are due to their own stupidity, and at other times they are due to the failures of others.

After David had conquered the Philistines, he desired to bring the Ark of God to Jerusalem. The Ark represented the presence of God among the people. David knew that it would be a holy, yet exciting day when he could bring the Ark back to Jerusalem.

David and all the house of Israel celebrated before the Lord with instruments, lyres, harps, tambourines, castanets, and cymbals. The only problem in this celebration was that no one knew how to properly transport the Ark. They had placed the Ark upon a new cart which was led by two young men. The oxen pulling the cart jarred it and a man named Uzza reached out his hand to steady the Ark. Immediately, God struck Uzza dead for his irreverence to the symbol of God's holy presence.

David and the priests should have known how to transport the

Ark. In Israel's history there were some sad examples of what had happened to people who had carried it incorrectly, the most dramatic of those being when Samuel was a child. More than 70 men had been killed for irreverence to the Ark. (See Num. 4:15 and 1 Sam. 6:19.)

Because of David's failure to know God's Word, Uzza died. When David realized what had happened, he became angry and then afraid of God and said, "How can the Ark come to me?" The celebration was disbanded and the Ark was left at the house of Obededom the Gittite. David had tasted failure, as all successful men frequently do.

David desired the presence of God. But with that desire, there is a price to pay. While God is Love, He is also Righteousness. Our heavenly Father is the Almighty God, the Holy One of Israel. We must approach Him with reverence and let that reverence saturate our daily lives.

Frustration and Persistence

One of the prices of success is persistence, and David had this. He also had the intelligence to find out how to transport the Ark. Some people think David was a genius. I don't have any real argument with that, but in this instance, I wonder: If he was so bright, why did it take him three months to figure out how to get the Ark back to Jerusalem?

When David heard that the people holding the Ark were being blessed, he promptly arranged a second attempt to transport the Ark to Jerusalem. And this time he did it correctly, according to God's Word. Again there was a day of music and dancing, and gifts were prepared for all the people.

Marital Tension

Marital strife is a price paid many times by a successful man and his wife. In the course of the festive day, as spirits rose, David began dancing vigorously before the Lord, so much so that he exposed himself to the young women in the crowd. He was not far from his house at the time, and his wife Michal was looking out the window and saw him. She didn't like what she saw any more than the average wife would today. In fact, she "despised him in her heart" (2 Sam. 6:16).

Some of us wouldn't dance vigorously about anything, while others would dance a jig at the drop of a hat. David was a very colorful man and he danced with all his might as he praised God for the safe return of the Ark.

I personally like quietness in worship, but there are people who like vigorous singing and clapping of hands. This is fine if their personalities are geared that way. We have to be careful not to criticize David in this instance, especially when we realize what happened to Michal for her attitude.

If you find that the singing, clapping, and enthusiasm in some churches is not to your liking, that's all right; but don't mock the person who appreciates it. Some Christians could stand a little more enthusiasm, while others might tone down a bit.

David, who had not seen Michal observing him through the window, took the Ark to its place in the tabernacle, and offered burnt offerings and peace offerings before the Lord. Then he blessed the people in the name of the Lord, and distributed gifts of bread, meat, and raisins to everyone.

When the ceremonies were over, David returned to his house to bless his own household. Michal greeted him with: "How glorious was the king of Israel today, who uncovered himself in the eyes of the handmaids of his servants, as one of the vain fellows shamelessly uncovereth himself!" (6:20, KJV)

Now David, the man after God's own heart, might be expected to take his bride in his arms and comfort her, quietly explaining why he had behaved as he did, so she would understand.

But that isn't quite how it happened. He came right back with, It was before the Lord, who chose me above your father, and above all his house, to appoint me ruler over the people of the Lord, over Israel; therefore, I will celebrate before the Lord. And I will be more lightly esteemed than this and will be humble in my own eyes, but with the maids of whom you have spoken, with them I will be distinguished (6:21-22).

I personally feel that Michal was out of order in jumping on David in this manner. She should have known that her husband was a very enthusiastic man, and should have recognized the significance of bringing the Ark back to Jerusalem. But instead, she cut him with sarcasm, as only a woman can do. I am an expert on this, having seven daughters and a bride. Sometimes acid seems to drip from those lovely tongues. We call it a "saber tongue" in our house, and often will say, "Slash him again! He is bleeding, but he is still standing."

Michal had no child unto the day of her death. We do not know if she was made barren by God, or if this conflict caused David to no longer have intercourse with her. Certainly, David had many other opportunities to satisfy his sexual needs, and he may have eliminated Michal from her physical function as his wife. Often the scars of caustic remarks are deep and long-lasting.

Disappointment

Many times the successful man is disappointed in life. David was no exception. After he was established as king, David had some time to reflect on the fact that God had given him rest from his enemies. He called Nathan the prophet to talk with him about an idea he had. David said, "See now, I dwell in a house of cedar, but the Ark of God dwells within tent curtains" (7:2). Nathan responded, "Go, do all that is in your mind, for the Lord is with you" (7:3).

David had a sincere desire to build a house for the Lord, but this was not God's plan for him. That night God spoke to Nathan, telling him to go to David and deny him the privilege of building the temple.

David had known great success as a man of war. Now, that military success was going to cost him something that he wanted very much. People who have multiple talents, as David did, are able to express themselves in many ways with great skill. We have already seen David as shepherd, soldier, musician, poet, leader, builder, and king. But now, God was saying "No" to a deep desire in David's heart. A successful man does not like to be told "No."

God's message to David through the Prophet Nathan expressed the following ideas:

• Did I ever ask anyone to build Me a house?

- I took you from the pasture to be the ruler.
- I have been with you, cut off your enemies, and made you a great name.
- I will appoint a place for My people, plant them, and give them peace.
- I will give you order and rest from your enemies.
- I will prepare a house for you, and give you eternal life.
- Your descendant will have your kingdom and I will bless him.
- He shall build a house for My name.
- I will be a Father to him and correct him and love him.
- Your house and your kingdom shall endure before Me forever.

The prophecy about David's kingdom concerned the immediate future and the distant future. There was promise of a son to succeed him, and there was promise of another Descendant, the Messiah, who would establish the throne of David forever.

When God says "No" to a successful man, it is part of His plan for that man's life. Every successful man should learn this lesson.

Prayer for the Future

When God says "No," He also says "Yes" to other possibilities. And David heard that "Yes." His prayer of response to God, in the face of this disappointment, is an example for Christians today. David sat before the Lord and said,

- Who am I, O Lord God, and what is my house, that Thou has brought me thus far?
- Thou hast spoken also of the house of Thy servant concerning the distant future.
- For the sake of Thy word, and according to Thine own heart, Thou has done all this greatness.
- Thou hast established for Thyself Thy people Israel as Thine own people forever.
- The word that Thou has spoken concerning Thy servant and his house, confirm it.
- For Thou . . . hast made a revelation . . . saying, "I will build you a house"; therefore Thy servant has found courage to pray this prayer to Thee.

- Bless the house of Thy servant, that it may continue forever before Thee. (See 7:18-29.)

David was truly a man after God's own heart. He wanted to live a life pleasing to God, even though he was disappointed that God had denied his plan to build the house of the Lord.

Commitment

Another price for success is total commitment. David was at peace with God. He knew that he was not going to build the temple. After a tremendous experience with God, and after accepting God's "No" in his life, the reality that he was king came crashing down on David's shoulders.

This is one of the costs of success: We have to meet the variety of challenges that confront us. There is no escape from our responsibilities. In our society, both men and women are managing many different roles as they deal with family, community, work, church, friends, school, and special interest groups. Within each of these roles, they are called upon to use diverse skills. In our age of specialization, it seems paradoxical that so much diversity is asked of each person in his daily life.

In 2 Samuel 8 and 10, battles are recorded which appear to be parts of the same story. David defeated the Philistines and took Gath and its towns from them. He also defeated Moab, and then divided the people into three parts, killing two thirds of them, and keeping one third as servants for Israel. (See 8:1-2.)

Then the king of the Ammonites died, and Hanun his son became king. David, remembering that King Nahash had shown kindness to him, and wanting in some way to console Hanun, sent his servants to Hanun with a message.

The princes of the Ammonites convinced Hanun that David's men were really spies coming in advance of an army. To humiliate them, the Ammonites took the servants and shaved off one half of their beards, cut off their garments at the hip, and sent them away. (See 10:3-4.) This caused great shame to David's servants, for the Hebrew man considered long hair a sign of his separation unto God.

When the sons of Ammon saw that they had alienated David,

they hired the Syrians of Bethrehob and of Zobah, as well as other mercenaries, in preparation for the war they thought would follow.

On hearing what had happened, David sent Joab and all his army to Ammon. Joab divided the soldiers, giving one half to Abishai, so that they could fight separately if necessary, and also come to one another's aid.

Joab's word to Abishai before the battle is appropriate for us in a time when great demands are placed upon us: "Be strong, and let us show ourselves courageous for the sake of our people and for the cities of our God; and may the Lord do what is good in His sight" (10:12).

Joab and his army defeated the Syrians, and when the sons of Ammon saw that the Syrians had fled, they also ran before Abishai and entered the city. Following this victory, Joab returned to Jerusalem.

The defeated Syrians gathered together, and Hadadezer brought his armies to Helam, in an effort to reestablish his power near the Euphrates River. Once again the Syrians suffered a terrible defeat. After this, each of the kings of the several states involved made his peace with David and served Israel. (See 10:15-19; 8:3-8.)

In 2 Samuel 8:4 we read that David hamstrung (hocked) the chariot horses belonging to Hadadezer's armies. To hamstring is to cut the Achilles tendon. This removes the power and push-off of the hind legs. The horses would not be totally crippled, but would lose power in the legs. They would be useful for farming, but no longer good for battle.

Fame

A successful man occasionally gains wide fame for his work. David made a name for himself, just as God had said he would. However, there was danger in this. Success has its own traps. This was not only true for David, but can be true for us as well. If you consider yourself a successful person, you need to pray that you will continually give your work and your successes to God. You came into the world with nothing, and you will go out with nothing!

The wrap-up on these battles must have taken a long time. David sent garrisons of men to Syria, and the Syrians became servants to David and brought him tribute. Also David took the shields of gold from Hadadezer's men and large amounts of bronze from surrounding cities to Jerusalem.

As a gesture of friendship, King Toi of Hamath, who was an enemy of Hadadezer, sent an envoy—his son Joram—to David to give greetings, congratulations, and a blessing. Joram brought gifts of silver, gold, and bronze, which David dedicated to the Lord.

No prominent person has ever achieved success solely by his own efforts. And in 2 Samuel 8:16-18, we read the names of the men who helped David command and rule. Joab was Commander, Jehoshaphat was recorder, Zadok and Ahimelech were priests, and Seraiah was secretary. Benaiah was over the Cherethites and the Pelethites, and David's sons were chief ministers. (See also 1 Chron. 18:17.)

Generosity

There are many opportunities for generosity in the life of a successful man. Now that David's kingdom had been established, he remembered the covenant that he had made years before with Jonathan. David asked whether there was anyone from Jonathan's family to whom he might show generosity. One of Saul's servants named Ziba told the king that there was a son of Jonathan who was crippled.

David sent for the young Prince Mephibosheth, who bowed before the king. David reassured him that he had no reason to be afraid, and that for the sake of his father Jonathan, David would restore to him all the land of his grandfather Saul. David also invited Mephibosheth to eat at his table.

Again Mephibosheth bowed low and said, "What is your servant, that you should regard a dead dog like me?" (9:8)

David advised Ziba that all which had belonged to Saul would be given to Mephibosheth, and that Ziba would work for him. Bringing Ziba into the work force added his 15 sons and their households and his 20 servants and their families. All of these people would be working the lands that had belonged to Saul.

Let's look at David's generosity. He had made a vow many years before, but now there was no one who remembered it. Yet David gave back a substantial amount of property to Mephibosheth because of the promise made to Jonathan.

You might think *Oh, David could afford to be generous. After all, he had so much.* But rich people are not necessarily generous. The reason for David's generosity was that deep in his heart he had committed his wealth to God. He was perfectly willing to return to Mephibosheth the property of his grandfather Saul, because it was part of a covenant made before the Lord.

In David's generosity to Mephibosheth, we see grace extended that reminds me of God's grace to us in Christ. David brought the young man into a relationship of restoration. But to Mephibosheth, this was something new, since he had never met David before. He didn't know of the covenant and love between his father and David. He was now being drawn into a love that had existed before he was born.

Mephibosheth would eat at the table of the king from that time forward. In Eastern cultures, eating at the table of another person suggests belonging, partaking of the freedom of the household. We, as Christians, are invited to come to the table that God has prepared for us, in the communion fellowship, as we partake of the spiritual gift of Christ crucified, risen, and ascended for us. We are drawn into a love that existed before we knew anything about it.

It is mentioned several times that Mephibosheth was lame. Many of us at times feel that we are lame. Some of us are lame in our feet and some are lame at the other end; but all of us have weaknesses. When we feel we aren't able to meet every responsibility, we must have confidence that God will provide, in His time and in His way.

This is a moving story of the grace of God, revealed in the life of David—a man after God's own heart—a man who knew the price one pays for success.

מָגֵן דָּוִד

8
David's
Mid-Life Crisis

2 SAMUEL 11—12

Although David's involvement with Bathsheba is well-known, we don't hear many sermons or read many books about the story, since people find it difficult to understand how this great man of God could sin so scandalously.

Yet, we are all aware that this sin occurs today in Christian circles among men of outstanding Christian commitment. Often these men, like David, are in middle age, and become involved with younger women. We could describe this as one of the results of the male menopause or mid-life syndrome. The sin of David is outlined for us in detail, to the point that it is almost embarrassing. We wonder how David, or any Christian man today, could be so careless, and risk losing his career and family for lusting after a woman.

The seventh commandment is, "Thou shalt not commit adultery," and the tenth is, "Thou shalt not covet thy neighbor's wife." (See Ex. 20:14-17, KJV.) In the Sermon on the Mount Jesus stated that if a man even looked upon a woman with lust, he had committed adultery in his heart. This sin is so serious that Jesus further stated, "If your right eye is causing you to offend, cut it out. If your right hand is causing you to offend, cut it off." In other words, He would rather see a man go through life a physical cripple than for him to fall into the sin of adultery.

We find David as a middle-aged man yielding to the passion of his sexual drives. Let's look at this familiar story, not to rationalize David's sin, but rather to see what lessons God has for us.

Break in the Routine

In the spring of the year, when kings traditionally went out to battle, David sent his general Joab in his place. On the day when this story begins, David had spent the afternoon in bed and had arisen in the early evening.

We might immediately connect the mid-life syndrome with David being in Jerusalem and in bed. However, in fairness, we need to recognize that it is impossible to run a kingdom—or a business—without delegating authority and responsibility. Sending Joab in his place was not necessarily an evasion of responsibility.

The fact that he was in bed might be explained by one of two things: the extreme heat in Israel during certain times of the year, or the possibility that David wasn't feeling well that day. All of us men who are, or have been, in middle age know there is mental adjustment necessary when we are no longer as physically vigorous as we used to be. Our legs are not as strong, or our reflexes as quick. When we take part in sports, we can't see the ball as well as we used to. Tennis players in middle age tend to hit a blur rather than a ball. Many men have great difficulty adjusting to this gradual decline in their physical strength.

David rose and went up to the roof of the palace to look at

the city that he was making ever more beautiful. It was spring; the sap was rising, David was in mid-life, and although he didn't know it, he was about to have a crisis.

As David looked down, his gaze was arrested by the sight of a beautiful young woman. He called one of his servants to inquire who she was. When the message came that she was Bathsheba, the wife of Uriah the Hittite, that should have been the end of the whole matter because she was a married woman. But David kept on looking and desiring and coveting until he took action. He sent for Bathsheba.

Situation Ethics

Being fully aware of the sinfulness of adultery, David deliberately chose to violate a command of God. How far do *you* go in violating the Word of God? Maybe you don't like that question, but we all have our personal leeway within which we *do* feel free to violate God's Word. Maybe you stop at looking, or lusting. Or maybe you don't stop there.

The commands were given as guides, as preventives against sin and tragedy. When you violate one, you are apt to go a step further and violate another, and pretty soon you are in so deep that another doesn't seem so bad. In fact, it frequently seems necessary to cover the first two, and you keep going until the judgment of God falls. Your life is spoiled in part, your family is hurt, the kingdom of God is harmed. Yes, God will forgive your sin, but you and your family may carry the consequences of that sin for the rest of your lives.

A man who has been in a penitentiary can be forgiven for what he has done, but his prison record will not be erased. He carries it with him to affect the course of his life from that time forward.

A Provocative Woman

What was Bathsheba doing bathing outside so that she could be so easily seen? She wasn't exactly faultless in this story. Beautiful young women should be very much aware of how provocative they can be to a man. It is well for parents to help daughters understand the bounds of modesty. In recent years, many rape cases have gone against the woman because a judge or jury got the idea that she was being provocative. While this is not always the case, there are women who do use their physical attractiveness to their own advantage, in unwholesome ways.

I know I may come across here like a chauvinist, but I have lived for more than half a century, and in other cultures too, and I am aware of how men act and think. Parents need to teach their daughters to behave themselves within the bounds of modesty and personal safety.

One evening one of my seven daughters, who was in high school at the time, came and presented herself before me in her usual bubbly way. She had on hip huggers and a halter, which left a great deal of flesh exposed.

"Where are you going, honey?"

"I'm going out with my boyfriend."

I replied, "Honey, you may get raped!"

There was an awful silence. She left the room, but I noticed when she and the boyfriend went out that she was wearing something more modest. Considering her age and personality, I believe she was innocent—not trying to provoke anyone. We owe it to young girls to see that they do not go out—especially in innocence —dressed as if they are looking for trouble.

When we bought CBs for our car, we were told that if you have trouble on the road, you can get on an emergency band and let it be known that you need help. Someone immediately came on the band and said, "Well, if your daughter is alone, she should say, '*We* are having car trouble,' not 'I am!' Otherwise, she might soon have a bunch of men around who aren't exactly interested in her car!"

If a sweet young thing says she is alone on a lonely road, she is asking for problems. You might get the feeling that there is a certain amount of animal in the human male, and I think that is true.

Lusting from the Rooftop

David saw Bathsheba. And you know about David—if there had been sexual olympics at that time, he would have won the gold medal. His sexual appetite was never going to be satisfied, no matter how many women he had.

There is little possibility that he knew Bathsheba well enough to love her. In other words, what we are talking about here is just plain lust.

In our society, sex and lust and love are often confused. A doctor friend of mine told me that one of his patients announced to him that she was in love with him. He took care of the situation with tact and humor. He looked at her and said, "Obviously, this is not love, because to know me is to love me, and you don't know me."

Many in our society think that casual sex is fun and exciting. But this is not God's way for people. He designed for a man and a woman to enjoy sexual love and fulfillment within the commitment of marriage.

Marriage Renewal

I find it interesting how many couples are renewing their marriage vows after 10, 20, or 30 years. This is good, but I think there is also another way. When a husband and wife come together sexually and in real love, they are reaffirming their wedding vows. On the wedding night, they are consummating their vows, and each time after is a pledge and renewal of those vows.

All of us who are married know the sacredness that sexual love can bring to a marriage. It is a sad fact that many people who are married no longer have much love for one another. Such people are likely to be influenced by current trends in our cuture. They feel trapped in a marriage that no longer offers emotional rewards. They feel there must be some other way to live. If they don't believe in divorce or have no particular reason to divorce, but have no sexual love fulfillment in the marriage, they are living with a time bomb. People like this—and there are many in the church —need to do something corrective, and not just sit there year after year, letting their marriages deteriorate still further.

There is so much writing today about the techniques of sex, as if it were some kind of machine that you learn to operate. I think what should be stressed is that the gift of sex is for mutual satisfaction and for expressions of love. It was not given for indulgence in lustful pursuits or meaningless bedroom gymnastics.

Springtime Dalliance

Bathsheba was with David for some weeks. This is suggested by reference to the ritual cleansing after her menstruation, both before she came to David and after she left him. The likelihood of her becoming pregnant was excellent, when you consider David's potency and the time of her cycle. The Levitical law was designed so that the women were in their fertile periods when they became ritually clean. Those Jewish husbands had a real problem! Every time their wives became available, they were also in the fertile time of their cycle. I read this and chuckle, wondering if David knew or even cared about menstrual and fertility cycles.

It is probable that David grew to love Bathsheba during these weeks, because in years following there seems to have been a real devotion to her. We can well imagine that she was the one who taught their son Solomon about the meaning of love, which he so beautifully expressed in his Song. Also, David seems to have been a better father to Solomon than to his other sons. There's scriptural evidence that David spent more time with him, sharing his wisdom and knowledge of God. In the Book of Proverbs, Solomon mentioned things that he had learned from his father. When David was on his deathbed, he was eager to honor the vow he had made to Bathsheba—that their son was to be the king.

David and Bathsheba sinned most seriously, and yet there can be no doubt that God blessed their marriage. To them He gave the son who would be king. To them He gave a lasting love, something that David apparently had not found with his other wives. And this offers hope today for people who have compounded error upon error, sin upon sin, in their mixed-up lives. God can take us where we are and lead us. If our intention from now on is to serve God, He will honor that intention.

This does not mean that we have an excuse to sin, just because God forgives and is gracious. Nor does it mean that we will escape the results of sin. David had no excuse to sin, nor did he escape the results. He paid dearly for his sin. He must have wondered later what ever possessed him to ignore the laws of God, and bring such tragedy on his family and the nation.

Premeditated Murder

After Bathsheba returned home, she sent word back to David, "I am pregnant." Now what was he to do?

Bathsheba's husband Uriah was one of David's men who had been with him in the wilderness wandering. David had had 30 mighty men and the last one on the list was Uriah the Hittite. Uriah had married the daughter of another of the 30 men, Eliam, son of Ahithophel.

David sent word for Uriah to come home immediately from the battle, hoping he would sleep with his wife, and perhaps miscalculate and accept as his own the child that would be born. Uriah came home, but being a man of duty and strength, he would not go to his wife while his comrades were at war. Possibly he smelled a rat, namely David.

When David asked him why he hadn't gone home, but had slept at the king's gate, Uriah answered, "The Ark and Israel and Judah are staying in temporary shelters, and my lord Joab and the servants of my lord are camping in the open field. Shall I then go to my house to eat and to drink and to lie with my wife? By your life and the life of your soul, I will not do this thing" (2 Sam. 11:11).

David asked Uriah to remain in Jerusalem for the next day, and that following evening David invited him for dinner and gave him so much wine that Uriah became drunk. David assumed that when Uriah was not in full control of his senses, he would surely go home. But he did not, giving support to the suggestion that Uriah was a better man drunk than David was sober.

The next day David sent him back to battle carrying a letter to Joab that arranged Uriah's death. When Joab had killed Abner, David had expressed that he didn't know what to do with his nephews. Joab now might have wondered what he should do with his uncle. Joab wasn't opposed to some killing here and there, but at least he did it himself. And he killed people he considered enemies for various reasons. Now David was asking Joab to arrange the death of one of the mighty men.

Joab could have refused, or could have appeared to comply and yet failed in the attempt to have Uriah killed. But for his own reasons, he went along with the scheme, put Uriah in front of the battle, saw that he was dead, and sent the message back to David along with the other news of the war. Joab had used poor battle strategy to accomplish Uriah's death. In the process he probably had endangered the lives of other soldiers.

If the king protested the poor strategy, the messenger was to tell David that Uriah was dead. David's answer, after hearing this, was sickening. He said, "Do not let this thing displease you, for the sword devours one as well as another; make your battle against the city stronger and overthrow it" (11:25). In other words, *Don't feel guilty, Joab. Let's just say that he might have been killed anyway. Use whatever strategy is necessary. The end can justify the means.*

David knew exactly what he was doing. Joab was well aware, as was Bathsheba, of what was happening—just as we are, when we intend to do wrong. But the most important factor is that God is fully aware of what we are doing. He knows the motives of our hearts. While we may be able to cover up our sins in the sight of other people, we cannot avoid the all-seeing eyes of God. David's great sin of adultery was compounded by premeditated murder. The consequences of this sin become very apparent as David's life unfolds.

After the time of mourning for her husband, Bathsheba was brought to the house of David to become his wife. And she bore him a son. But what they had done displeased the Lord.

Some ladies of my acquaintance believe that Bathsheba was a neglected wife who fell prey to a nasty old man. She may have been neglected and unappreciated. We don't know. But her circumstances do not lessen or excuse her sin.

Sin Rebuked

The Lord sent the Prophet Nathan to tell David a story about a poor man who had only one lamb. A neighboring rich man had many flocks but he was greedy. When a houseguest came to stay, and the rich host needed a lamb for dinner, he didn't want to slaughter one of his own, and took the lamb belonging to the poor man.

After hearing the story, David angrily asked, "Who is this rich man? Surely he will die."

Nathan bluntly replied,

You are the man! Thus says the Lord God of Israel, "It is I who anointed you king over Israel, and it is I who delivered you from the hand of Saul. I also gave you your master's house and your master's wives into your care, and I gave you the house of Israel and Judah; and if that had been too little, I would have added to you many more things like these!

"Why have you despised the Word of the Lord by doing evil in His sight? You have struck down Uriah the Hittite with the sword, have taken his wife to be your wife, and have killed him with the sword of the sons of Ammon. Now therefore, the sword shall never depart from your house, because you have despised Me and have taken the wife of Uriah the Hittite to be your wife. . . . Behold, I will raise up evil against you from your own household; I will even take your wives before your eyes, and give them to your companion, and he shall lie with your wives in broad daylight. Indeed you did it secretly, but I will do this thing before all Israel, and under the sun" (12:7-12).

David's immediate reply was, "I have sinned."

And Nathan answered, "The Lord also has taken away your sin; you shall not die. However, because by this deed you have given occasion to the enemies of the Lord to blaspheme, the child also that is born to you shall surely die" (12:13-14). And then Nathan left.

Right now you may be relating to David or to Nathan. If you are a David, and a Nathan comes to you with the warning and rebuke of God, be sure to listen to what he says, considering the possibility that he may truly be sent by God.

If you relate to Nathan, then be very sure that it is God who is sending you to challenge or rebuke a Christian brother or sister. If you believe it is God, then be sure to go prayerfully.

On one occasion, I had the experience of being a Nathan. I was asked to talk with a pastor, by his own family who was very concerned about him. I was much younger then and didn't really want to go, but I did, and told him that I had been sent by his family to challenge him about his behavior. He did not react initially as David did, but instead became very angry. What I was really saying to him was, "Thou art the man."

I asked, "I have been told that you did thus and thus. Is it true or not?"

That was the end of his anger, as he began to realize that God was dealing with him and his sin. He repented and was given many more years of ministry in another location. That pastor died with his boots on, just exactly the way he wanted it to be. God can use a penitent sinner in His work.

While I am thankful that situation turned out the way it did, I still remember what an unpleasant task it was for me to go to him. I believed then, and do now, that God does on occasion send His people to try to bring wayward servants of His back into line—back into fellowship.

As children grow older, they at times play the part of Nathan for their parents. Not every sin is like David's. Many sins occur within a normal family circle and parents move out of balance one way or another. They need the chiding of one who loves them, to get them in line again.

Why do you think David became so angry at the rich man of the story? Have you ever noticed when someone becomes terribly angry about another's fault, he frequently has a similar problem himself? It is common for each of us to overreact to the same thing of which we are guilty. Often, the things that bug us the most in our kids are the very weaknesses we recognize in ourselves.

The Wages of Sin

David reacted as a guilty person: "The man shall die!" Deep in his heart he knew he was guilty. This is indicated by Nathan's response that David wouldn't die but that the child would. Someone had to die for the enormity of this sin, for David had given the enemy of the Lord opportunity to blaspheme.

Notice, Nathan didn't just barge in to David and say, "You are guilty. You are the man." No, he prepared him emotionally first by telling him the story. When David was angry at the sin, then Nathan reminded him of God's abundant blessings on his life.

The reason the child would die was that David had caused God's name to be blasphemed by His enemies. This is a serious offense against a Holy God. The Apostle Paul quoted Isaiah 52:5 —"For the name of God is blasphemed among the Gentiles because of you" (Rom. 2:24). He was speaking to those who had a double standard of behavior. They taught one thing and did another. Paul wrote to Timothy about Hymenaeus and Alexander whom Paul had "delivered over to Satan, so that they may be taught not to blaspheme" (1 Tim. 1:20). What was their sin? They had rejected faith and a good conscience, and had suffered shipwreck in regard to their faith.

The child was born to David and Bathsheba and after some months became ill. The suffering of the child was probably not nearly as severe as that of David and Bathsheba, who were losing a child they loved, and were in remorse over their sins.

During the seven days that the child was seriously ill, David fasted and prayed, and may have conceived the thoughts of Psalm 51. When his servants saw him lying all night on the ground, they were afraid that he was deranged and might harm himself. David noticed their concern and heard their whispers about him. He asked, "Is the child dead?"

Upon learning that he was, David arose from the earth, anointed himself, changed his clothes, and came into the house of the Lord, not to express bitterness, but to worship.

The principle of prayer comes through very clearly. In the midst of anguish and suffering, God expects us to come to Him in prayer and worship. We can do as David did, if we recognize the Almighty and Eternal God who is in control of all circumstances.

What Is Appropriate?
I think the order of David's actions is interesting. He arose from the earth, washed and anointed himself, and changed into clean clothes before going into the house of the Lord. We struggle a bit

in our culture with the casualness of our teenagers as they go into God's house. In times past it was routine to dress in our finest for worship services. We felt that it was not appropriate to go into the house of God without washing and putting on clean clothes. Young people in particular seem to feel that it is all right to "come as you are."

I recall with fondness an episode from our family's life. When I was an elder at the Wheaton Bible Church, our pastor decided to serve communion one Sunday evening in a rather unique way. Several tables were set with bread and grape juice, and the members could participate at any table they chose. An elder was assigned to each table.

On taking my place to serve, I noticed a group of rather motley-looking kids at the back of the sanctuary. Recognizing that they were mine, I felt delighted they were in church and were coming to the communion table I was serving. However, as they came closer to the table, I saw that my older son was dressed in a purple shirt that looked like a gunny sack. His hands were stuck deep in the pockets of his blue jeans. Directly behind him was my delightful teenage daughter in hip huggers, with an exposed umbilicus. One other youngster was in cut-off jeans, and all seemed to have come to the service "just as I am."

Well, this father's heart was divided at that moment. I was delighted that my children were there and taking communion, but I was not exactly happy with their attire. Later, when I challenged them about being in the house of the Lord dressed like that, I used the old cliche, "Would you go to see the president of the United States without first getting all dressed up in the appropriate clothes?" One daughter looked at me with big blue eyes and quietly said, "It depends, Daddy, on how well I knew the president."

Acceptance of God's Will

After worshiping in the house of the Lord, David went to his own house, sat down, and ate. David's behavior again concerned his servants. They could not quite figure out why he would fast and weep while the child was alive and then arise and eat after the child was dead. David's deep conception of God and his acceptance of God's will comes through in his words: "While the child was still alive, I fasted and wept; for I said, 'Who knows, the Lord may be gracious to me, that the child may live.' But now he has died; why should I fast? Can I bring him back again? I shall go to him, but he will not return to me" (2 Sam. 12:22-23).

David, a man after God's own heart, accepted the will of God over and over again during his life without complaint. In his psalms he poured out a heart that burned for the things of God, a heart that truly desired to please God.

A Gift from God

David comforted his wife in the loss of their son and she conceived and bore a son whom they called Solomon. And the Lord loved Solomon and sent word through Nathan the prophet of another name for the baby.

This was almost too much to believe. This couple had sinned, had lost one son as a result, and now knew that there was hardship predicted because of what they had done. And yet when this baby arrived, and was already named, special word came from God Himself expressing His great love for the child and His gift of another name, *Jedidiah* or *Beloved of the Lord.*

If David and Bathsheba had been in one of our 20th-century churches, they would probably have been drummed out of the corps. But God doesn't work that way in people's lives. He forgives and then blesses those who have sinned. If He didn't, there would be no hope for any of us. It is so easy for us to forget that we are sinners. But our wrong behavior and our thoughts are no surprise to God. It is pleasing to Him when a person has a lifelong desire to serve and love Him, as David did.

In evangelical circles, we too often glibly remark that when a person is born again, he becomes a new creature in Christ, and that all things become new. But we don't always act as though we believe this truth.

David and Bathsheba could have destroyed their lives and their effectiveness spiritually. But it seems that they made their hearts right with God. Their past was behind them. The product of their adultery was taken home to heaven, and now life was starting anew.

There are so many people today with very sordid pasts, and praise God, they can become new creatures. God can use them, if the desire of their hearts is to please Him.

Back at the Battlefront

Joab, who had been sent off to fight against the children of Ammon at least two years earlier, was still fighting. Now he sent messages to David, saying that he had finally been successful in taking the City of Waters, and David should come quickly to claim the victory. The character of Joab again comes through in a positive manner. He was concerned that if he claimed the victory, the soldiers would name the city after him—rather than after David.

David listened to the suggestion of Joab, gathered the people together, fought against Rabbah, and took the city. David claimed the conquered king's crown, which was made of a talent of gold with precious stones. He also claimed great spoils in abundance from the city. The people of the city became servants to the children of Israel.

As David with all the people returned to Jerusalem, he was now the victorious king of Israel, reigning in the city of God. God had permitted him to prosper in the spoils of his campaign, and had also permitted him to become the father of a son whom God particularly loved. King David, a man after God's heart, was serving a God of great mercy and great love.

מָגֵן דָּוִד

9
Dealing with
Wild Children

2 SAMUEL 13—16

One weakness in David's character was his inability to deal with
his grown-up sons in a positive manner, especially when a problem
arose. Children up to the age of six or eight years can respond
to a father who loves them and gives them consistent discipline.

However, when children move into their teenage years, a
father must use caution and good judgment about becoming
involved in their lives. Allowing increasing freedom from parental
guidance is easier said than done, as I can well affirm at this stage
in my own family life. However, when an adolescent is violating
a civil or spiritual law, then obviously it is the father's responsibility to deal with the problem as quickly as possible and as

severely as necessary. It is the teenager's responsibility to recognize the father's actions as proper and appropriate.

Amnon—Lovesick!

In 2 Samuel 13, a tragic series of events begins, involving David's adult children. By this time he had had 19 sons and 1 daughter by his multiple wives. (See 1 Chron 3:1-9.) He also had children by his concubines, but we are not told their names or how many there were.

The main characters in this story are Amnon, David's first son; Absalom, his third son; and Absalom's full sister, Tamar. Absalom and Tamar were children of Maacah who was daughter of Talmai, the king of Geshur. As far as we know, these were the only children of David with royal lineage on both sides. The fourth character was Jonadab, David's nephew, and cousin to David's children. The four were involved in a spicy story that would make a good script for a modern soap opera.

Amnon was probably considered the future heir to the throne, and this makes his behavior all the more serious. He fell in love with his younger sister Tamar who was a very beautiful young woman.

Amnon was so lovesick that he lost weight and became bedridden. Jonadab, trying to be helpful, said, "Why don't you ask your father to send Tamar over to prepare some food for you in your room?"

The Bible calls Jonadab a shrewd man, and his plan *was* shrewd. Amnon's dilemma was two-fold. He didn't particularly want to marry Tamar, although there is indication that he could have asked permission of David to do so. He merely lusted after her.

Also, on two counts he would be violating the Jewish law if he lay with her. There was a prohibition against taking a virgin (Ex. 22:16-17; Deut. 22:28-29), and a law against taking one's own sister or half sister (Lev. 20:17; 18:9, 11; Deut. 27:22).

Jonadab figured he would help Amnon get her into the room and Amnon could take it from there. In thinking about these young people, we need to remember that David had multiple households. They would not all have grown up together as brothers and sisters do today. Tamar and Absalom had the same mother, but the other sons all had different mothers, and would not have been with Tamar on a day-to-day basis.

Amnon thought his cousin had a great idea, and asked David to send Tamar in to prepare a meal in his sight that he might eat from her hand. To me the lesson in what happened is rather clear. One of David's weaknesses was his eye for the ladies, and Amnon was simply a chip off the old man's block. I would think that David, being as hot-blooded as he was, would have easily recognized that Amnon's request—for a fair, young thing fluttering about his house preparing a meal—would stimulate more than his physical appetite.

However, David did not suspect this, or at least did not prevent it. He sent Tamar over to Amnon's house to fix the desired meal.

I also see what happened as associated with David's own sin. These young men had grown up in the environment of their father's wandering eye. What Amnon proposed to do was not as serious as what David had done with Bathsheba. The penalty of the Law for lying with a married woman was stoning for both. The penalty for lying with a virgin was either marrying her or paying the dowry price.

Tamar—Raped!

Amnon had one thing on his mind, his lust for Tamar. He thought he was in love, but what followed was not the action of one who truly loves. He may have started out with some sort of love, but he ended with pure lust. It is pretty hard to say that any man who forces himself on a woman loves her at that moment.

Tamar came in and prepared the food he wanted, and then Amnon sent everyone else away. When he made it clear that the two of them would take the food into the bedroom, you would think that she might have suspected something. This suggests that Tamar must have been very trusting of her brother, and yet old enough to know the facts of life and the penalties for violating the law.

As soon as he made his intentions clear, she objected: "No,

my brother, do not violate me, for such a thing is not done in Israel; do not do this disgraceful thing! As for me, where could I get rid of my reproach? And as for you, you will be like one of the fools in Israel. Now therefore, please speak to the king, for he will not withhold me from you" (2 Sam. 13:12-13).

Tamar gave Amnon several good reasons for not pursuing what he wanted to do, but he refused to listen. She would marry him if he wanted, and his willingness to marry her would have been some proof of love.

Amnon paid no attention to Tamar's words, but forced her to lie with him. Certainly, here we see an entirely different situation than the one with David and Bathsheba. Bathsheba had been indiscreet in exposing herself while bathing. Also, there was no indication that she was an unwilling partner. Tamar seemed to be entirely innocent and made every effort to avoid the action. The blame falls squarely on Amnon for his lustful violation of his sister.

This story suggests the emotions of rape. After the act, Amnon hated her exceedingly: "So that the hatred wherewith he hated her was greater than the love wherewith he had loved her." Amnon then said, "Arise, be gone" (v. 15, KJV).

It is not uncommon, when a man has had sexual relations with an unloved woman, for him to have this sense of disgust with himself and also with her. It is also not uncommon for a man to beat up on a woman with whom he has been involved sexually, and this is true even though he has forced himself upon her. The Word of God is very practical in its application, and in its exposure of the human heart. Casual sex—sex without love and commitment—may be temporarily exciting, but it is not satisfying, and leaves very much to be desired.

Absalom—Outraged!

Again Tamar tried to persuade Amnon to take her as his wife, but he would not listen to her and simply cast her out. Her response was to put ashes on her head, tear her princess garment, and weep openly. Absalom, her older brother, immediately sensed what had happened, and asked if Amnon had been with her. We see the manliness of Absalom as he took his younger sister to his home, attempted to comfort her, and then spoke to his father about the incident.

Absalom did not speak to Amnon from that point forward, and hated his older half brother because of this rape.

When King David heard of what had happened, he was very angry. But the Word of God does not tell us that he did anything about the problem. In fact, two full years passed before any further mention was made of the situation. This left Absalom in the position of being the only adult male who seemed to care about what had been done to Tamar.

Certainly David, as father of the man and woman involved in this unfortunate affair, should have taken action. He was the king of Israel. Amnon was the heir apparent. The wrong cried out for fatherly and kingly action. David, however, apparently did nothing.

Few of us as fathers will have such a serious problem in our homes. However, the lesson I see is this: When one of our children either plans to break or has broken laws, then it is our responsibility to warn him, and enforce cooperation with the law. We must warn our young people that even if they are simply accomplices to a crime, they will pay the full price according to the law of the land. Unfortunately, some "successful" fathers attempt to get their children off the hook, rather than making it abundantly clear to them they will be held responsible to the law for their behavior. David was one of those fathers who could not be realistic when a son had obviously broken the law.

Amnon—Murdered!

The consequences of David's failure are exposed in the latter verses of 2 Samuel 13. After two full years, Absalom planned a family gathering. It was sheep-shearing time, and Absalom asked all 17 of David's sons to be his guests for the feast. He also asked David to come, but the king declined. Absalom urged his father, but David was adamant, although he did bless Absalom.

When David had suggested that they should not all go to Absalom's house, Absalom had especially asked for Amnon to attend. David's response was, "Why Amnon?" Again he did not seem to realize the potential danger in his son's request. It seems incredible that David would not have recognized Absalom's hatred for his older brother, or have known that the two young men had not spoken to one another for two years.

Absalom planned quite a party, and told his servants to see that Amnon got plenty to drink. Then when Amnon was drunk, Absalom would give the signal and the servants would strike.

What Absalom was doing was the reverse of what David had done. David had killed Uriah so that he could have the woman. If Bathsheba had had a brother to defend her, he probably could have struck out at David. Absalom was moving now against the violator of his sister, and in the process was rebuking his father. Absalom seemed to have a higher standard than David did. If the father would not protect the honor of the daughter, at least he, her brother would.

A wild rumor circulated that Absalom had slain all of the king's sons. This rumor caused David to tear his garments and lie on the earth. Again Jonadab appeared on the scene to assure David that only Amnon was dead, and that this was by the appointment of Absalom from the day that Amnon had raped Tamar.

The following scene, as all of David's sons lifted up their voices and wept along with the king and all of his servants, exposes the emotional grief of David and his family for this tragic event.

Absalom fled to his grandfather, the king of Geshur, staying there for three years. During this time David mourned every day for him, and longed to go to Absalom but did not do so.

This story clearly illustrates the problem some fathers have in dealing with their children in times of grief, or when reconciliation is indicated. It is so important to deal with problems and to do so promptly. David longed to go to Absalom for reconciliation, but did not. He was angry with Amnon, but did not take action. Fathers should be challenged by this story to recognize and prevent these major problems in their families, and to respond in a manner which will prevent, as much as possible, the tragic consequences of sin. Again, may I emphasize to teenagers the necessity of recognizing their fathers' responsibility to interfere in their lives when tragedy becomes a possibility.

David—Persuaded to Reconciliation

As 2 Samuel 14 opens, Absalom had been in Geshur for three years. Joab, the loyal general of David, perceived the king's heartache for Absalom and came up with a plan to help David understand his error. Joab asked a wise woman from Tekoa to go to David in mourning apparel and tell him a story about her two sons. Her story was similar to that of Absalom and Amnon, in that one brother had killed the other. The whole family was demanding the death of the murderer. The woman further pleaded that the Jewish law about the avenger of blood be bypassed. David quickly recognized the seriousness of the situation and agreed with her that the life of her son should be spared. The wise woman of Tekoa then challenged David that he was doing exactly the same thing in banishing Absalom from the land of Israel.

She further appealed to the king, inferring he was like an angel of God, and wise according to the wisdom of God to know all things that were in the earth.

By this time David realized that Joab was probably behind this scheme and asked the woman if this were not so. David also recognized his error and told Joab that he should go and bring Absalom back to Jerusalem.

Joab's response was heartwarming. He fell to the ground, bowed before the king, and thanked David for this decision. We see something of the way in which these two men related to each other, in Joab's effusive words to David: "Today your servant knows that I have found favor in your sight, O my lord, the king, in that the king has performed the request of his servant" (14:22). At least three different times in their long association, David unsuccessfully tried to replace Joab, but Joab was always there trying to find favor in the sight of his uncle.

David decreed that Absalom could return to his own house in Jerusalem, but he could not look upon the face of the king.

It may seem strange, at first glance, that David would respond so quickly to a fabricated story told by a woman dressed in mourning clothes. But human experience shows that many times we can help others much more easily than we can solve problems in our own families. Professional counselors do this all the time. They often can see problems in other families, but have difficulty recognizing when something is wrong in their own. Businessmen do well to find investment counselors to manage their money. They are more successful with the money of strangers than with their own. For a similar reason, physicians rarely treat their own families. They are so emotionally involved with their children that medical decisions concerning them are most difficult.

Absalom—Excluded!

David's restriction on Absalom, permitting him to return to his home in Jerusalem but not to look on his father's face, suggests that David was not fully reinstating Absalom into his former position of father-son relationship. The opposite of love is not hate, but rather indifference. David was now showing Absalom a considerable amount of indifference, which could be crushing to him as a son. It may well explain Absalom's subsequent behavior.

Some fathers today are too busy in their daily pursuit of success. They crush their children, not by hating them, but by being indifferent toward them. Though the father may be physically present in the home, his sons and daughters seldom see his face. This type of rejection can lead to all types of bizarre behavior in a young person. To outsiders it seems incredible that "such a fine Christian family" could have a son or daughter who behaves this way. However, someone counseling with the young person will often find a situation similar to Absalom's, in which the child is suffering because of a father's neglect—"Absalom shall not see my face."

In this story we have a description of Absalom's physical beauty. He had no blemish from the sole of his foot to the crown of his head, and his hair was so plush that it weighed three pounds after his annual haircut. Americans have just gone through a fad of long hair, and those of us who lean toward Archie Bunker are distressed when our sons' earlobes are covered, let alone their collars. We can imagine the unusual appearance of Absalom, with such a huge head of hair.

We are also told that Absalom had three sons and one daughter, a beautiful young lady whose name was Tamar, again indicating Absalom's deep relationship with his sister Tamar.

For two full years Absalom lived in Jerusalem, but did not see his father's face. Finally, Absalom took matters into his own hands in an attempt to gain reconciliation with his father. Absalom sent for Joab, but the general would not come. He sent word another time and still Joab failed to come. So Absalom simply ordered Joab's barley field to be set on fire, and that brought immediate response!

What a sad thing to see a young man who literally has to set fire to a field in order to gain attention! The abnormal behavior of many young people today is simply a desperate attempt to gain attention from those they love. This is a sad commentary on the failure of many parents.

In this case it was Joab, an adult, to whom this young man turned, hoping to gain help. Again, you and I are held responsible in the eyes of God for all the young people in our acquaintance, in our church family as well as in our own individual families. We are to be sensitive to their needs, and recognize that sometimes they are literally crying out for help and attention from adults whom they love and respect.

Reconciliation

Finally, Joab responded to Absalom and went to King David to intercede for him. The young man was so desperate that he had pleaded with Joab, "Let me see the king's face, and if there be any iniquity in me let him kill me." Absalom was willing to lose his life in order to see his father's face. Do you see the desperation and the tragedy in this young man's life? Do you see the power of a father's indifference upon the son's personality and behavior pattern?

Absalom came to the king, bowed his face to the ground before him, and then finally, David kissed Absalom. What a lesson to learn! It took David five years after Absalom had killed Amnon to finally reconcile himself to his son—three years of banishment to a foreign land, and two years of exile from his father in Jerusalem.

We must be very careful as parents that we are not so slow to learn this extremely important lesson. If a young man or young lady is acting in a very objectionable manner, consider seriously whether he or she is crying out desperately for attention and for reconciliation. As parents we should not force ourselves upon a child who does not want reconciliation. But, as so beautifully told to us in the story of the prodigal son, once that son came to his senses and returned to his father's house, the father greeted him with kisses, robes, rings, and immediate restoration of sonship in the family. Fortunately, David, through the insistence of his son and his faithful friend Joab, finally came to his senses and responded to the desperate attempts of Absalom for reconciliation.

It would be nice to say that after they had kissed and made up, they lived happily ever after. But life just does not unfold that way, and the story of David doesn't either. From that point forward, Absalom rebelled against his father, driving David out of Jerusalem, and eventually losing his own life. In David's lamentation for his son Absalom, his mourning and his grief are heartrending. In honesty we have to wonder if this intense grief was motivated by true love, or a sense of guilt. Whatever David's motive, the consequences of sin—of David's macho lifestyle and his failure to rule his household—are very apparent.

David was not called a man after God's own heart because of his talent or ability, but rather because of his readiness to repent. David was a man after God's own heart because he wanted to live a life that pleased God. Unfortunately, he had a character and a personality that made this desire most difficult to fulfill.

Because David's life is recorded in such honesty, you and I can learn about the love and grace of God. As penitent sinners, we come to the Father, asking for reconciliation. He quickly greets us with open arms, and kisses us and places us in a position of complete restoration in the family of God. We can look into His face and cry, "Abba, Father," because He is our Father through our relationship to His Son, Jesus Christ, our Lord and our

Saviour. Woven through the life of David is the grace of reconciliation, and the power of the Spirit of God, which is available to anyone who penitently desires to be reconciled to God.

David—Betrayed!

Second Samuel 15 describes Absalom's rebellion against his father. He provided himself with an official chariot and horses, along with 50 men to run before him. These were signs of assuming royal power, and would be impressive to people who favored him. In addition to this, he rose up early each morning to be by the gate of the city greeting people, and attempting to resolve their problems on behalf of the king. Absalom was not only handsome, but a real public relations man. If anyone came near to him to do him obeisance, Absalom responded by putting forth his hand, taking the person and kissing him. In this manner, he won the hearts of the men of Israel.

Many people feel that the practice of medicine is a science, but I feel it often is more art than science. Many years ago I was told by a very fine physician that it was vitally important to touch each patient. People respond positively to the human touch. I have faithfully incorporated this into my practice, both in my office and in the hospital. Sometime during the consultation, the patient is touched by the physician's hand.

At a county hospital, an old man was diagnosed as requiring elective surgery for removal of his gall bladder. He agreed to sign the permit for surgery only if "the tall, gray-haired doctor" would do his operation. The intern dealing with the patient asked that the right doctor be pointed out. It was the chief of surgery. When asked why he chose this particular doctor, the old man shrugged his shoulders and said, "Each day when all you doctors come into the ward, he is the only one who touches me. He pinches my toe."

Yes, the touch of the human hand is very important in human communications. Absalom knew this. He touched and kissed each person he dealt with at the city gate. It is little wonder that Absalom stole the hearts of the men of Israel.

After two years of this public relations campaign, Absalom

went to King David, asking permission to leave Jerusalem to return to Hebron. "Please let me go and pay my vow which I have vowed to the Lord, in Hebron. For your servant vowed a vow while I was living at Geshur in Syria, saying, 'If the Lord shall indeed bring me back to Jerusalem, then I will serve the Lord.'" David responded to this by saying, "Go in peace" (15:7-9).

Absalom was not going to repeat his vows to the Lord, but was going to set up the beginning stages of his reign, with a network of spies throughout the nation. Two hundred men accompanied Absalom from Jerusalem, but they were not aware of what their leader was planning.

I am sure you have had situations in which people have spiritualized their motives to you. David was really taken in by the request of his son to pay a vow to the Lord. Jesus warned in the Sermon on the Mount that we are to be aware of false prophets who go about in sheep's clothing. And in Christian work today, we meet people who are insincere in their actions, though their words certainly seem to pledge allegiance to the Lord.

One other very significant person joined Absalom at this time. Ahithophel the Gilonite, David's counselor, father of one of David's mighty men, and grandfather of Bathsheba, received word that Absalom wanted to see him. The conspiracy against David grew strong, for "the people increased continually with Absalom" (15:12).

David—Grieved

Once David was informed that the hearts of the men of Israel were following Absalom, he elected to leave the city of Jerusalem, asking all of his servants and their families to go with him. In fact Jerusalem was left completely unoccupied, except for 10 concubines who were deliberately left behind to keep the palace.

We must read this account carefully to see the full impact. David, the king of Israel, was abandoning the holy city of Jerusalem in fear of his son. The heartbreak of this man is very apparent, and yet even in his suffering, we still see his excellent qualities as a man and as a king.

As David was leaving the city, he expressed his concern for Jerusalem. "Go in haste, lest he overtake us quickly and bring down calamity on us and strike the city with the edge of the sword" (15:14). Jerusalem, the city of God, was very important to David. He was concerned that if he remained in Jerusalem, Absalom would come by force and ruin the city.

As they came to the edge of the city, David stood aside and let all the people pass by him. One man caught his attention, Ittai the Gittite. Despite his heartbreak, David was aware of how Ittai must have been feeling and said to him: "Why will you also go with us? Return and remain with the king, for you are a foreigner and also an exile; return to your own place. You came only yesterday, and shall I today make you wander with us, while I go where I will? Return and take back your brothers; mercy and truth be with you." Ittai already felt great loyalty to David and answered, "As the Lord lives, and as my lord the king lives, surely wherever my lord the king may be, whether for death or for life, there also your servant will be" (15:19-21). And so Ittai continued on with the fleeing people. The entire company was in great sorrow, weeping with loud voices on their way to the wilderness.

David was also concerned about the Ark of God, and decided that it should remain in Jerusalem. He appointed Zadok, one of the priests, to carry the Ark back into the city. Then in a magnificent statement, he expressed his confidence in God: "If I find favor in the sight of the Lord, then He will bring me back again, and show me both it and His habitation. But if He should say thus, 'I have no delight in you,' behold, here I am, let Him do to me as seems good to Him" (15:25-26). In his depths of despair, David still recognized that God was in control of his life. His confidence was in God.

In his actions and words, David was also saying that Jerusalem belonged to God and that the Ark was the symbol of God's presence in Jerusalem. He, David, was the temporary one, the dispensable one. David knew that as long as he was absent from the city, there would be little reason for warfare or destruction of the city.

Then David asked the priest, "Aren't you a seer?" Remember when David was a fugitive and he and the priest asked of the Urim and the Thummin the pleasure of God? The people might not have done this as frequently in subsequent years. David was suggesting to the priest that he consult the Lord and then let David know the result.

David however was not only a spiritually oriented man. He was also the king and a military leader—a man's man of his time. In addition to asking Zadok and Abiathar to carry the Ark back into the city, David was also aware that their two sons had set up a grapevine of communication by which they could relay information back to the king. David had confidence in God, but he was also using his own ingenuity, anticipating the battles that would lie ahead. Although it might seem that David was exercising little faith, I believe God expects us to use our minds and our abilities as much as possible. He expects that our motives will be honorable, and that the desires of our hearts will be to live in a way that pleases Him. There is no question in my mind that David's heart was right with God, although many times his decisions and behavior left a great deal to be desired.

The poignant scene that follows is touching to any father of rebellious children. "David went up the ascent of the Mount of Olives, and wept as he went, and his head was covered and he walked barefoot. Then all the people who were with him each covered his head and went up weeping as they went" (v. 30). What a scene of mourning—David, the king of Israel, the heartbroken father, walking over rough terrain and in a very hot climate. To walk barefoot and to cover his head demonstrated profound sorrow and mourning. This was a scene of true grief, portraying the price David was paying for his failure to rule his house properly.

As David stood on the mountain weeping, someone informed him that Ahithophel, his counselor, was with Absalom's conspirators. David said, "O Lord, I pray, make the counsel of Ahithophel foolishness" (v. 31).

Just as David was coming to the top of the mountain, Hushai the Archite approached him, with his coat torn and with dust upon his head. David asked Hushai to return to Jerusalem and pose as a servant to Absalom. "Say to Absalom, 'I will be your servant, O king; as I have been your father's servant in time past, so I will now be your servant,' then you can thwart the counsel of Ahithophel for me" (v. 34).

He also revealed to Hushai the grapevine of communication arranged with Zadok and Abiathar. The loyalty of these men to David was very significant. There are few men who are able to attract and maintain such loyalty, especially in times of adversity.

David—Reviled!

While David was still walking about the mountain, a little past the summit, he met up with Ziba, the servant of Mephibosheth. Ziba's donkeys were carrying 200 loaves of bread, 100 clusters of raisins, 100 summer fruits, and a jug of wine. Ziba said that all this was for the king. When David inquired where Mephibosheth was, Ziba answered that he had stayed on in Jerusalem in hope that the throne would be given to him that day. Just as Ziba had hoped, the king said, "Behold, all that belongs to Mephibosheth is yours" (16:4). This was quite a profitable exchange—a bit of food for an entire estate.

David had passed over the peak and was now making his way down the Mount of Olives to the city of Bahurim, when he encountered yet another man, Shimei, who was from the house of Saul. This man came forth cursing, casting stones, and shouting at David, calling him a bloody man and a worthless person. David's past seemd to be catching up with him. Shimei said, "The Lord has returned upon you all the bloodshed of the house of Saul, in whose place you have reigned; and the Lord has given the kingdom into the hand of your son Absalom. And behold, you are taken in your own evil, for you are a man of bloodshed!" (16:8)

David's nephew Abishai responded, "Let me go over and cut off his head." But the king refused this helpful suggestion, saying, "If he curses, and if the Lord has told him, 'Curse David,' then who shall say, 'Why have you done so?' " (v. 10)

David also said to Abishai and to his servants, "Behold, my

son who came out from me seeks my life; how much more now this Benjaminite? Let him alone and let him curse, for the Lord has told him. Perhaps the Lord will look on my affliction and return good to me instead of his cursing this day" (vv. 11-12).

What an outstanding statement of forgiveness! In the Sermon on the Mount, Jesus taught that Christian character does not permit retaliation. He said that if we are struck on the right cheek, we are to turn the other also. If we are asked to go one mile, we are to go two. Christ was saying that God is in control of the Christian's life, and that vengeance is in the hand of God. During this very emotional climb on Mount Olivet, a lesser man than David could well have taken delight in seeing Shimei's head separated from his shoulders.

Absalom—Advised

The scene now shifts to Jerusalem where Absalom, with the men of Israel, was in the palace. Ahithophel, David's counselor, was there with Absalom as his advisor; Hushai the Archite had also arrived as a secret representative of David. He was so convincing that he had become part of the inner circle of Absalom's counsel of war.

Absalom said to Ahithophel, "Give your advice. What shall we do?" (v. 20) Ahithophel had a plan which would clearly establish Absalom as the new ruler of Jerusalem. He suggested that Absalom go into the concubines whom David had left behind, and that he do this in plain sight of the people of the city. This would demonstrate, he said, "that you have made yourself odious to your father. The hands of all who are with you will also be strengthened" (v. 21). According to Jewish custom, this would be an outward sign that Absalom had completely broken with David, and the men of Israel would have a clear choice for king.

They pitched a tent for Absalom on the roof, and he went into the concubines of his father, in the sight of all Israel. This action was a fulfillment of the punishment predicted by the Prophet Nathan after David's sin with Bathsheba. (See 2 Sam. 12:11.)

One final word about Ahithophel. In the last verse of chapter 16, we find a commentary about this man: "The advice of

Ahithophel, which he gave in those days, was as if one inquired of the Word of God; so was all the advice of Ahithophel regarded by both David and Absalom."

Ahithophel was well acquainted with Jewish law and custom, and had prided himself on offering advice which was recognized as very wise. Unfortunately, Ahithophel could not cope with the rejection of his counsel, as we shall soon see.

מָגֵן דָּוִד

10
Violence
and Sorrow

2 SAMUEL 17—20

Violence has played a large part in the story of David. The violence has been usually directed at someone who could be termed "the enemy." The most significant exception was Uriah. However, in this section, there is more personal violence involving people who are not enemies, than in any other part of David's life. He personally was not responsible for the acts, but he was involved through his men.

Ahithophel, who formerly had been David's wise counselor, was now advising Absalom in Jerusalem: "Please let me choose 12,000 men that I may arise and pursue David tonight" (17:1). His plan was to come upon David when he was weary and weakhanded, and kill him. Then he would bring back all of David's troops so that they could serve under Absalom.

This was wise counsel and it pleased Absalom and all the leaders of Israel who were present. Wanting a second opinion, Absalom said, "Call Hushai the Archite also, and let us hear what he has to say" (v. 5). You will recall that Hushai was the friend of David who had been sent to bring the counsel of Ahithophel to foolishness.

When Hushai came into the room. Absalom told him what Ahithophel had advised, making it very easy for Hushai to make another suggestion. He promptly stated that the counselor's advice was not good for this occasion. He reminded Absalom that David was a valiant man, and the men with him were mighty men of war. David would not be sleeping with his troops but would be alert to danger. Hushai also counseled that if this attack were to fail, it would be reported that there had been a slaughter among Absalom's followers.

Hushai suggested that Absalom call all the men of the nation to war, from Dan to Beersheba, and then personally lead them against David. With this kind of strength, even if David retreated into a city, Absalom would have enough men to literally draw the city down into a valley.

Absalom and the leaders of Israel decided this advice was better than Ahithophel's. But notice the second half of verse 14: "For the Lord had ordained to thwart the good counsel of Ahithophel, in order that the Lord might bring calamity on Absalom."

You might wonder if it was right for David to send his friend Hushai to spy on Absalom and lie to him. Couldn't David just have prayed and asked the Lord to bring Ahithophel's counsel to foolishness and let God take care of it? Why did David have to interfere? Why would he endanger his friend's life?

While we can't accurately judge David's motives and actions, it is clear from the Word of God that the Lord permitted all of this to occur, so that evil might come to Absalom. Though this may seem hard to understand, it does bring to mind the story of Job. Satan who moved to and fro on the earth, presented himself before God, along with the other sons of God. This suggests that God is truly in control of Satan. As the story of Job unfolds, it is apparent that God permitted Satan to touch Job, but always with limitations.

Although this particular incident between Hushai and Absalom did not involve Satan per se, it did involve the control of God over the actions of man. While God gives man free will, and does not usually interfere in men's acts or in the results of their acts, at times He does intervene to accomplish His own purposes.

When we hear that every knee shall bow at the name of Jesus, (Phil. 2:10), we don't always fully appreciate that idea. We don't like the notion that "it is appointed for men to die once and after this comes judgment" (Heb. 9:27). But whether we like it or whether we understand it, God is ultimately in control of every situation. No man truly controls his own destiny.

Deception

Hushai, following David's instructions, sent Zadok and Abiathar, the priests, to tell David not to spend the night at the fords of the wilderness, but rather to cross over and remove himself from danger. Unfortunately, the young men were seen on their way, and a woman hid them in the mouth of a well to deceive Absalom's servants who were pursuing the young men. To protect them, the woman lied, "They are gone over the brook of water." When Absalom's men had left in search of them, the two ran to where David was, delivered the message, and David crossed the Jordan with all his people.

Suicide

Meanwhile, Ahithophel was considering the fact that his advice had not been taken. He, who gave counsel like the Word of God itself, saddled his donkey, went home, put his house in order, and strangled himself. He was buried in the grave of his father. This suicide was not done in momentary anguish but was a premeditated act.

I find this entire incident difficult to understand. Deceit and lying were used to accomplish the purpose of God, although we certainly cannot claim that God willed this approach. We don't know Ahithophel's reasons for transferring loyalty to Absalom; but as a man with a reputation for wisdom, he must have thought his reasons were sufficient. He found it difficult to understand and accept that his counsel was rejected for the plan of someone else. Possibly he realized that he was now in a position to serve neither David nor Absalom.

The lesson I learn from this story is there is no substitute for honesty and forthrightness. We need to be transparent people, with no deceit in our lives. And no covering up. We need to face life head-on, with confidence in God who understands all things.

Also, Ahithophel seemed to be an opportunist, and an ambitious man in pursuit of power. The man of God has no business pursuing power for its own sake. If it comes as a by-product, you need to know how to handle power, and the only way I know to do this is to keep your feet on the ground, and your priorities straight before God. If you have power, and are out of fellowship with God, you are in trouble spiritually. A successful man whose priorities are wrong can exaggerate a minor failure, as Ahithophel did, until he even considers suicide.

Provisions for David

While David and his men traveled to Mahanaim, Absalom crossed the Jordan with his army in pursuit of his father. He had appointed a man named Amasa over the army in place of Joab, which suggests that most of David's army were now following Absalom. Amasa was a cousin to Absalom, the son of David's sister Abigail.

Three men, Shobi, Machir, and Barzillai, brought provisions to David and his people: beds, basins, pottery, wheat, barley, flour, parched grain, beans, lentils, parched seeds, honey curds, sheep, and cheese of the herd. They had said to themselves, "The people are hungry and weary and thirsty in the wilderness" (2 Sam. 17:29).

The backgrounds of these three men are interesting to note. Shobi was from Rabbah, which had been captured by David. (See 2 Sam. 12:26, 29.) Machir was the man with whom Mephibosheth was staying when David found him. (See 2 Sam. 9:4-5.) Barzillai was an old man whom we will meet again, in this chapter and in chapter 12.

God often sends provisions to us through other people, and He sends provisions to them through us. We need to be sensitive to the needs of other people and to the voice of God, so that we are ready to provide for someone who is hungry and thirsty and weary.

Listen to Advice

David numbered his people into hundreds and thousands and then divided them into three groups, naming as captains, Joab, Abishai, and Ittai the Gittite who had demonstrated such loyalty to David.

David's plan was to lead his army personally, but the people felt that he was too valuable to risk his life in this way. They said to him, "You should not go out; for if we indeed flee, they will not care about us, even if half of us die, they will not care about us. But you are worth ten thousand of us; therefore now it is better that you be ready to help us from the city" (18:3).

David replied, "Whatever seems best to you I will do" (v. 4).

I remember when I taught this portion of 2 Samuel to our Homebuilders' class. That morning before we went to church, I talked with my bride about the lesson I had prepared. As I shared my excitement about some of the ideas with her, she said, "I hope you practice what you preach!" That took the wind out of my sails a bit, but I probably deserved it.

What had prompted her to make such a remark was the lesson I drew from David's readiness to do whatever the people decided. I had said to Janet, "We must learn to listen to other people."

If a person is going to be a leader, he should learn to listen to the advice of others. David was fully aware of his kingship under God. He was confident that God was in control of the people of Israel, and of his own life. Yet he was willing to hear what others had to say. In our lives we need to be willing to listen to our children, spouses, employees, and friends.

At one time my wife and I had a difference of opinion that lasted several days. Two of our daughters realized things weren't quite normal at home. You might say you could have cut the tension with a knife. In her usual uninhibited way, one daughter said,

"Hey, Dad, what's going on between you and Mom?"

I said, "I'm not mad at her, but she is mad at me."

The girls then asked why, and I mentioned our difference of opinion. To my surprise both of them said, "Dad, you are too hard on Mom. Lay off!"

They added a couple of comments I won't mention. I must say though that I was really impressed that these two teenagers would tell me that they were siding with their mother—even though deep in my heart I knew she was wrong. But I listened to them, and decided *maybe* they were right after all. (Maybe I *was* too hard on her.)

When we were in Africa, a mother brought in a child whose one leg was shorter than the other. After X rays were taken, I examined the child, and talked with the mother through an interpreter, She said, "There's something wrong with the hip joint."

I looked at the X rays, but they didn't include the hip joint. My first thought was, *What does this village woman know about orthopedics?* Fortunately, I examined the child carefully, and sure enough, he had a dislocated hip. That Kikuyu mother, who had never even seen an X ray before, had correctly diagnosed the problem.

In medicine we're taught to listen to the patient. He is well aware of what is wrong. Maybe you've been in a doctor's office explaining your problem and feeling annoyed because he is writing notes all the time. You get the impression he isn't paying much attention to you. I've tried to solve this by having a nurse with me at all times to write the notes I need. This way I can watch the patient as he is telling his story. It's amazing what you can learn if you watch and listen carefully.

When my children talk to me, I look at them, to *hear* what they are really saying. Often their words alone don't convey what I hear. From the expressions on their faces, and the gestures of their bodies, I try to decide what they want to communicate to me.

Hung by His Hair

As the people went out to war, David stood at the gate, and the people heard him say to the commanders, "Deal gently for my sake with the young man Absalom," (18:5). Everyone knew that Absalom's life was to be spared. In the ensuing battle, 20,000 men died, as the servants of David prevailed in a treacherous setting—"The forest devoured more people that day than the sword devoured" (18:8).

Absalom had personally led his men and had escaped injury in the battle. As he was riding through the forest on his mule, he failed to see a great oak tree directly in front of him. His mule ran under the spreading oak and the branches secured themselves in Absalom's thick hair. The mule went right on, leaving Absalom hanging helplessly.

When the servants told Joab what they had seen, the general asked, "Why didn't you cut him down and kill him? I would have given you a reward—ten pieces of silver and a belt."

One servant answered, "Even if I should receive a thousand pieces of silver in my hand, I would not put out my hand against the king's son, for in our hearing the king charged you and Abishai and Ittai, saying, 'Protect for me the young man Absalom!'" (18:12)

The next verse is an insight into both David and Joab. The servant said that nothing was hidden from David; and that if he had struck down Absalom, Joab himself would have acted as if he didn't have any knowledge of it.

Joab's reaction to this was a curt, "I will not waste time here with you" (18:14). Going to where Absalom was hanging, and finding him still alive, he took three spears and thrust them through the young man's heart. Then 10 of Joab's armor bearers struck Absalom, to administer the coup de grace, after which Joab blew the trumpet of victory to end the battle.

They took Absalom's body and threw it into a deep pit in the forest and built a mound of stones over it. Seeing what had happened, Absalom's army fled to their tents.

Absalom had been concerned about a monument by which people would remember him. How different his burial was from what he would have wanted! He said that he had no son to preserve his name. We know that he had had three sons, but they may have died or been estranged from their father.

When we studied this lesson together in Homebuilders, one of our members said that when we die, we can leave either a monument of what we have accomplished in our work, or the heritage of good children. A few people seem to leave both, but most of us have to make a choice, either to pursue success as the world defines it, or to concentrate on what is really important and be relatively unknown by the world.

There is no question that raising a bunch of kids involves great effort, but the rewards and joys go beyond explanation. I really don't know what life would be like without children. However, good parenting means that the young child is consistently disciplined in love, that the older child is taught to honor father and mother, and that the father continues to love and be involved with his children. When this is done, in most cases, the children will be delights and not demons.

My heart aches when patients express how much they dislike their own teenagers. My teens are just as noisy and crazy as anybody else's, but I certainly don't have that feeling of dislike for them. Rather, Janet and I are delighted with them. If we can keep communication lines open with them, then it is a privilege to talk with our kids and help them resolve their problems. To see them develop into mature men and women who can take responsibility, follow instructions, and show respect for leadership is reward enough.

Absalom wanted a pillar to memorialize himself. I am not interested in a pillar, but rather want to leave a legacy of godly leadership to my children, so they in turn will be able to make contributions to their world in the future.

A Father's Anguish

Since there were no radios or telegraph systems in David's world, the communications had to be handled by runners. Ahimaaz, son of Zadok, asked Joab if he could take the news to David. Joab said, "No, you are not the one to take this news to the king." Joab then turned to a Cushite, asking him to run to King David and report what had transpired.

Ahimaaz pleaded with Joab to permit him to run also. Joab

finally gave in, and Ahimaaz ran by way of the plain, and outran the Cushite.

David was sitting between the two gates when a watchman reported that a man was running alone. David was sure a man alone had good news. However, the watchman saw another man coming. Still the king was sure the second one had good news. When the watchman identified the first man as Ahimaaz, David was certain he would bring a favorable report (18:24-27). We see here a father hoping against hope that his son is alive, desperately wanting to believe that the news will be good.

Ahimaaz arrived and fell on his face before the king. But when he was asked for the news, he was evasive. The message had to be delivered by the Cushite whom Joab had sent. The Cushite arrived shortly and David asked, "Is the young man Absalom safe?"

The Cushite blurted out, "The enemies of my lord should be as that young man." The good news, victory in battle, was totally lost on David in his sorrow for his son. He went to a chamber above the gate and wept. "O my son Absalom, my son, my son Absalom! Would I had died instead of you, O Absalom, my son, my son!" (18:33)

Those who have lost grown children can relate to David in his anguish over Absalom. Imagine, however, the guilt as well as the grief of David as he realized that part of Absalom's rebellion was due to his own inability to relate to his son, who for five years had been banished from his father's presence. It is no wonder that David cried out for his son, and even desired that he would have died instead of Absalom.

The closest I have come personally to this type of experience was in May 1978. My older son was traveling by car to Dallas to be married 10 days later. A few hours after he had left for Texas, our phone rang and a very kind voice said, "Dr. Jorden, this is the emergency room at Pontiac Hospital. Your son is here and has been in an accident."

There was a long pause that seemed like two or three hours to this dad. My heart was pounding. She went on to say, "He is still alive, but has been seriously injured."

For several hours the outcome was unsure; but thanks to God, my son survived and is in good health today. It is difficult for me to imagine what my grief would have been if had he died. Possibly I too would have cried out to God that I would rather have died in his place.

Shortly after that, the son of friends was killed in an accident. We were able to relate, at least partially, to their anguish and grief. There is a fellowship in suffering. People are comforted by the understanding of others who have been in a like situation.

Sometimes the failure to raise children properly ends in a tragedy that can almost be anticipated. I recall being at my hospital one afternoon when a teenage boy was brought in by ambulance. The boy had attempted to run across a four-lane highway and had gone into the pathway of a truck traveling at full speed. There was no way the driver could stop and the boy was killed instantly.

I overheard the nurse talking kindly with the father by phone, asking him to come to the hospital, since his son was in the emergency room. The father's response was interesting: He asked if it were his son Bob and the nurse said, "Yes." The father then asked, "Is he dead?" The nurse, with the tremendous compassion of emergency room nurses, answered, "I'm sorry—he is."

The father said, "I will come immediately." When he came to identify his son, the nurse asked him why he would think it was Bob. The father shook his head saying, "I just haven't been able to gain control over this boy. I knew he eventually would be killed." A tragic end to a father-son relationship much like that of David and Absalom.

Priorities

None of us wants to stand by the casket of a child, and in guilt and grief cry out, "My son, my son!" God has entrusted to us the care of our children. We are to teach them to obey the Lord and to obey their parents. We are not to provoke them to wrath, but to bring them up in the fear and admonition of the Lord. (See Eph. 6:4.) But how do we do this?

We need to think in terms of our priorities. For Christian men, the first priority is to want to live a life that is pleasing to God.

This means that you must find the time to pray and study the Word of God. No matter how busy your life, you must find time to do this, if you are to be a godly man.

Our second priority as Christian family men is to our wives. Here again we can consider David, with all the domestic problems he had. If you have trouble with just one wife, imagine the hassles David had!

We men are instructed in Ephesians 5 to love our wives. We are to love them as our own selves, love them as Christ loved the church, and love them sacrificially. When a man loves his wife this way, there is an atmosphere around the house which kids can relate to. It gives them a foundation to build on. They can see the relationship between father and mother. I know that this is so from my own experience—my wife is the most important person on earth to me.

When our youngest daughter was seven years old, one day she was giving her mother a very hard time. I learned of this and took her into the bedroom. I said to her, "Honey, I understand you were giving your mother a really hard time today."

She said, "Yes."

I said, "You give her a hard time quite often, don't you, but you don't do this to your dad. Why is that?"

She replied in an innocent way, "Because Mom isn't as big and strong as you are."

I answered, "You know, Honey, in the eyes of God, Mom and I are one person. So I want you to know, whenever you start to give her a hard time, that standing right behind her is this big strong fist!!!"

You should have seen her big blue eyes open even wider as she said, "Ohhhhhh." I think she got the point.

Our children need to understand the relationship between their parents. When we men love our wives the way God wants us to, our children see that one and one are one. Then they will respond accordingly.

Our next priority is to bring up our children in the fear of the Lord. This means that we will read the Scripture with them and pray with them, as well as using informal times to talk together.

I can remember my grandfather, who was a preacher, handling the Bible with great love. You could see by the way his hands touched that Book how he felt about it. This kind of attitude rubs off on children. We men are to lead our children in worship and devotions. And ladies, don't take out the garbage, clear the table, or write the grocery list while this is going on. If both parents don't have time to sit down for family devotions, how can you expect this time to mean anything special to your children?

Also, you need to make the devotions practical, asking questions of your children about what you read. Sometimes it is amazing to watch the look in their eyes and see absolutely nothing registering there. When this happens, repeat, "Now, this is what I just read, and I want to read it again." Then try to tie the lesson in with current events.

How often do your children see you reading the Word of God? I think it is very important for children to see their fathers and mothers reading the Bible. If they don't know that you read it, how can they relate to what you tell them about the authority of the Bible?

As we see this very touching scene of David crying out from his broken heart and wishing he had died for Absalom, I can only say, *There is no way you can die for your son if you are not willing to live for your son.* David did not live for Absalom.

David with the People Again

When Joab heard that the king continued to mourn for his son, he realized that the victory was turning to sadness for all the people. They were moving through the city quietly, trying not to be seen, instead of returning as victors.

Joab came right to the point with David—he was very blunt. He told the king that he had covered the faces of his servants with shame. Then Joab said to David, "You hate those who love you and love those who hate you. If Absalom were alive, it would be all right with you if all of us were dead. Now get up, go out, and speak kindly to your servants, because if you don't, they will all leave you and you will be worse off than you were before." (See 2 Sam. 19:5-7.)

Once again, David listened to Joab, and went to sit in the gate of the city with the people. We have admired Joab before, even while recognizing his faults. And in his actions here, we can see that at times a leader must quite bluntly admonish a superior, if his behavior is hurting the work of God. This takes a great deal of courage and prayer. However, if our motive is to enhance the work of God, then God will honor our courage.

An Invitation to Return

In 2 Samuel 19:8-9, we read, "Now Israel had fled, each to his tent. And all the people were quarreling throughout all the tribes of Israel." They were arguing about what they would do concerning David, and what he would do to them, if he came back as king. They all had supported Absalom, and now felt that they should bring David back into Jerusalem.

David sent a message to Zadok and Abiathar to speak to the elders of Judah, asking them why they were so slow in bringing back the king. David wanted to remind Judah, "You are my brothers, you are my bone and my flesh. Why then should you be the last to bring back the king?"

The priests were also to deliver a message to Amasa, David's nephew who had been Absalom's commander. "Are you not my bone and my flesh? May God do so to me, and more also, if you will not be commander of the army before me continually in place of Joab" (v. 13).

With these messages David turned the hearts of the people of Judah toward him, and they sent word to the king, saying, "Return, you and all your servants" (v. 14).

It is interesting to see that David, a valiant and strong man, asked for an invitation to return to Jerusalem, rather than re-occupying the throne by force. Even though we commended Joab for challenging David, there are other times when we need to await an invitation, rather than to move in with force. The Christian life is a life of balance. We find ourselves constantly evaluating the situations we face, to determine whether we are to wait upon the Lord, or to take action right away. If we are prayerful and careful in our motives, then God will honor us with guidance.

Four Men

David traveled from Mahanaim to Gilgal. The people of Judah crossed the Jordan to Gilgal in order to escort David home.

As David made his way back to Jerusalem, he encountered four men who had been a part of his life. The first was Shimei, who had abused David not long before. He came with the men of Judah to meet David, and fell down before the king saying, "Let not my lord consider me guilty, nor remember what I did wrong on the day when you came out from Jerusalem, for I know that I have sinned. For this reason I have come today, the first of the house of Joseph to meet you" (19:10-20).

Abishai said, "Shouldn't we kill him because he cursed the Lord's anointed?" The previous time, Abishai had offered to cut off Shimei's head. (See 16:9.)

David, being a man familiar with penitence, said to Shimei, "You shall not die." Shimei was certainly worthy of death, but David spared his life. As one who truly repented of his own sins, David could easily relate to Shimei, and forgive him for his behavior.

The second man mentioned was Ziba, the servant of Saul and Mephibosheth. He arrived with 1,000 men of Benjamin and his 15 sons and 20 servants. They rushed to the Jordan before the king, and crossed back and forth across the ford to bring over the king's household. David's last encounter with Ziba had been on the Mount of Olives, when Ziba had accused Mephibosheth of disloyalty to David.

The third man was Mephibosheth himself. He came to David disheveled, unshaven, with dirty clothes unchanged from the day David had left the palace. David asked him, "Why didn't you come with me, Mephibosheth?"

He answered, "Oh my lord, the king, my servant deceived me. I had intended to go but he slandered me to you. However, do now whatever you think is good. For all my father's household was nothing but dead men before my lord the king; yet you set your servant among those who ate at your own table. What right do I have yet that I should complain any more to the king?" (19:26-28)

According to the law, the land of a traitor became the property of the king, for him to dispose of as he wished. Ziba had accused Mephibosheth of being a traitor, and now Mephibosheth accused Ziba of slander. David quickly decided that the two could divide the land. Again we see David's generosity; he really didn't need to give either of them anything.

The fourth man to meet David was Barzillai, who was now 80 years old. He had come to escort David over the Jordan River. Barzillai "had sustained the king while he stayed at Mahanaim, for he was a very great man" (19:32). David invited him to come back to Jerusalem where David would care for him in his old age. Barzillai, however, was facing old age realistically. He admitted that he had difficulty discerning between good and evil, even had a hard time tasting what he ate or drank, and that his hearing was impaired as well. He knew that he would be a burden to the king, but agreed to walk a little way over the Jordan with David.

Barzillai had given generously to David in the past, and without any strings attached. This is shown by his question, "Why should the king compensate me with this reward?" (v. 36)

Some of my friends are rather wealthy Christians who support God's work generously. Occasionally, one will demonstrate a tendency to control an organization or a person whom he is supporting with tithes and offerings. In other words, the gifts have strings attached. If things are not going as he desires, the gifts are withheld in an act of retaliation and power.

Barzillai did not need to control David or exert his power. He simply asked that he go a little way with the king, and then turn back to his own city where he could die and be buried near the grave of his mother and father. Surely this grand old man had lived a full life, with a sincere heart and great contentment. General MacArthur said during World War II, "Only those who are not afraid to die are not afraid to live." This is so true.

After all the people had crossed over the Jordan, David kissed Barzillai and blessed him, and the old man returned to his home. As David proceeded to Jerusalem, he was accompanied by Chimham, a servant of Barzillai, with a promise that David would do good to Chimham for Barzillai's sake.

More Trouble

You would think that now all would be well. But the story just
does not unfold that way. For there was strife between the people
of Judah and Israel, as they continued to argue about David's
loyalty to each group. The men of Israel came to King David and
inquired why the brethren of Judah had stolen him away, along
with all of David's men. The men of Judah responded that David
was a kinsman of theirs, and asked why the men of Israel were
angry. Had the people of Judah eaten at the king's expense or
received gifts from David? The men of Israel responded that they
had 10 parts in the king, and thus had more right to David than
the one tribe of Judah. " 'Why then did you treat us with con-
tempt? Was it not our advice first to bring back our king?' Yet
the words of the men of Judah were harsher than the words of
the men of Israel" (19:43).

In the crowd was a worthless man by the name of Sheba, a
Benjaminite. During all this fussing, he suddenly blew a trumpet
and called out, "We have no portion in David, nor do we have
inheritance in the son of Jesse; every man to his tents, O Israel!"
(20:1) With this, all the men of Israel left David and followed
Sheba, so that David entered the city of Jerusalem escorted by
the tribe of Judah.

The contention between the men of Judah and the men of Israel
reminds me of squabbles within the church. Sometimes fierce
words are spoken to the point that we wonder what gets into these
men. But a positive lesson from this story is, that though the men
of Judah spoke more fiercely, they were also more loyal to David.
Many times those who speak more fiercely, in the church squabbles, are those who feel very strongly about the issue at hand.
I think we should hear people out, when they speak strongly, considering the possibility that their loyalty is well-founded and their
point well-taken.

After David arrived at the palace, he took the 10 women who
had been defiled by Absalom and placed them in confinement.
He maintained them but "did not go in to them. So they were
shut up until the day of their death, living as widows" (20:3).

These concubines had done nothing wrong and yet they had to

bear the penalty for Absalom's sin. Many of us have seen similar situations in life, where being in the wrong place at the wrong time has resulted in a person suffering a long-standing consequence that seemed undeserved.

Difficulties continued to plague David and his men in reestablishing the kingdom. Amasa, David's nephew and captain under Absalom, became captain under David. David instructed him to call up the men of Judah and to appear with them in three days. When Amasa took longer than the three days, David sent Abishai out with the king's servants to find Sheba.

Joab was available, but David was no longer using him. However, when Abishai took Joab's men to find Sheba, Joab went too, along with the Cherethites and the Pelethites (2 Sam. 8:18), and all the mighty men.

When they arrived at the large stone at Gibeon, Amasa came to meet them. This was the place where Abner and Joab had pitted their men against each other (2 Sam. 2:13). It was also the place where Abner had killed Joab's brother Asahel, and Joab in retaliation had killed Abner.

In a similar fashion as he had done to Abner, Joab walked up to Amasa to greet his cousin, grasped him in the customary way— by the beard—to kiss him, and drove a sword into the fifth rib killing him instantly.

There are some medical details in this gruesome story. First, driving a sword into the fifth rib would cause sudden death, since the heart is directly in that area. In addition, Joab struck a strong blow, for he hit him just once and Amasa wallowed in his own blood and inward parts that poured to the ground. Now that might seem almost impossible; but if a sword is thrust violently into the fifth rib with a downward stroke, the abdomen would be opened, and the inward parts would fall out almost immediately. The opening of the heart would cause excessive bleeding, and this, along with all the intestines, would certainly be a sight that would stop even the most mighty men in their tracks. In fact, it is the "mighty men" we watch most closely when we give shots or remove sutures, for they are the ones most likely to faint! One day a huge athlete lay on the floor of one of my examining rooms for several minutes, recovering from the news that he would have to have surgery on his thumb!

Joab and Abishai started after Sheba, but some of their men were unable to move after this gory murder. One of the young men tried to rally them by saying, "Whoever favors Joab and whoever is for David, let him follow Joab." Amasa still lay wallowing in his blood in the middle of the highway. This young man realized that no one was going to move very far until Amasa had been removed from sight. He pulled the body over to the field and covered him with a garment. Then all the men left to pursue Sheba.

Joab and the men found Sheba in a city called Abel Bethmaacah and cast up a mound against the city trying to get in. As Joab attempted to batter down the walls to get Sheba, a wise woman who lived in the city cried out to Joab inquiring if he was trying to destroy the city. He said he was only interested in Sheba. The woman promised that Sheba's head would be thrown to Joab over the city wall.

The woman then went to the people of the city and told them what they would have to do to save their city. Sheba's head was cut off, thrown over to Joab, who then blew his trumpet and dispersed the troops.

Joab returned to the king in Jerusalem and was reinstated as commander of the army of Israel. I think it is amazing that David didn't completely get rid of Joab. He was the one man who knew the truth about Uriah's death. He had also been responsible for the death of Absalom. After several attempts to replace him, David now let Joab continue as commander of the army, until David's impending death when he gave instructions to Solomon to do away with Joab. But for now, at least, Joab was safely home.

Teamwork

There is no such thing as a one-man show. An organization or kingdom cannot be run by one person. At the end of 2 Samuel 20, there is a listing of the people who helped David run the kingdom: Joab, Benaiah, Adoram, Jehoshaphat, Sheva, Zadok, Abiathar, and Ira the Jairite.

מָגֵן דָּוִד

11
Judgment—
Yet Praise

2 Samuel 21—24

We come now to a time in David's life of looking backward to the past as well as looking ahead. Chapters 21—24 include wars, famine, hangings, a psalm, a prophecy, a roll call, famous deeds, a severe pestilence, and the purchase of a threshing floor on which to offer a sacrifice to stop the pestilence.

There is question about when some of these events occurred, but since the writer of 2 Samuel chose to put them in this order, we will look at them as they appear. There are lessons for us in this unusual series of stories and verse.

Famine Because of an Old Sin
I find this first story difficult to understand. There was famine in the land and David went to the Lord to ask Him why. The Lord

said, "It is for Saul and his bloody house, because he put the Gibeonites to death" (21:1).

Were people suffering, hungry, and dying because Saul had sinned a long time before? Yes, and the nature of his sin brings another puzzle to the story. He had slain the Gibeonites because of his zeal for the house of God. He had thought he was doing a righteous act in killing sinners.

In spite of his zeal, Saul was in error because the people of Israel had given their oath to the Gibeonites to protect them. (See Joshua 9.) As king of Israel, Saul was responsible to keep all covenants which had been made by previous leaders.

David called the Gibeonites and asked what he should do for them. "How can I make atonement that you may bless the inheritance of the Lord?" (2 Sam. 21:3)

Throughout the Old Testament, Israel was called the "inheritance of the Lord." What David was really saying was, "I know that you are not part of the people of God, and you feel that we have wronged you. What can I do so you will want to bless Israel, rather than have feelings of animosity?"

David was telling them, "As the people of God, we have not lived up to our own laws in our relationship to you, and now we want to make this right."

This is a challenging thought to the people of God at any time in history! We should behave toward unbelievers in such a way that they will want to bless us rather than curse us. It means that we need to live with integrity, and honor all previous agreements. This applies not only to individuals and family units, but also to churches and religious organizations. I feel sad when I hear of churches or religious groups who don't pay their bills, or use questionable measures to obtain services or materials for less than the going rate. God's work should be beyond human reproach.

The Gibeonites explained that Saul had intended to fully eliminate them. However, they did not want money in retribution, nor did they want a mass killing. They asked for the lives of seven of Saul's sons or grandsons. David agreed to their demand. The seven were to be hanged before the Lord in Gibeah.

David chose the two sons of Rizpah who had been Saul's concubine, and the five sons born to Merab, Saul's daughter, and gave the seven to the Gibeonites, who hanged them on the mountain before the Lord. Some versions of Scripture say that the five sons were Michal's, and it is thought that she adopted and raised them after Merab died.

After the seven were dead, Rizpah grieved openly, spreading sackcloth from the rock for herself, and remaining out in the open with the bodies to guard them. She did not permit the birds to rest upon them by day, nor the beasts of the field by night, and she stayed there until the rains ended the famine.

We see here the profound grief of a mother, losing two sons because of the sins of the father. The consequences of sin fall not only upon the sinners, but often upon the children of sinners. As the first king of Israel, Saul was responsible to maintain a covenant made with the Gibeonites.

When David heard of Rizpah's vigil, he took the seven bodies along with the bones of Saul and Jonathan, and buried them in the grave of Kish, Saul's father.

The Bible leaves no question that the famine was the judgment of God upon the land for the disobedience of one man. Even though we may have made an agreement with someone under false pretense on his part, or an agreement that proved unwise, it is nevertheless a covenant and is to be upheld. There is no way to rationalize breaking promises we have made. In the Sermon on the Mount, we are warned by Jesus not to make oaths or covenants easily or carelessly. God will hold us responsible for our words.

A King Past His Prime

The second story in verses 15-22 is about a war with the Philistines, and is repeated in 1 Chronicles 20:4-8. In this battle, "David went down and his servants with him; and as they fought against the Philistines, David became weary" (2 Sam. 21:15).

Then Ishbibenob, a giant whose spear weighed more than 12 pounds, decided to kill David. But Abishai helped David, striking Ishbibenob and killing him. "Then the men of David swore to him, saying, 'You shall not go out again with us to battle, that you may not extinguish the lamp of Israel' " (21:17).

Following this were two more wars with the Philistines, one at Gob and one at Gath. One of the soldiers from Gath was a very large man who had six fingers on each hand and six toes on each foot. This orthopedic anomaly is still not uncommon, and has a strong tendancy to be repeated in a family.

Song of Deliverance

The entire chapter of 2 Samuel 22 is David's song of deliverance to God. This is not the song of a youthful and idealistic poet-musician, but of a gnarled veteran of many wars. He was a mighty man of valor who had been bruised and bent, but not broken.

In this beautiful song, David's heart cried out the identity of his Lord—my Rock, my Fortress, my Deliverer, my Shield, my Salvation, my Tower, my Refuge, and my Saviour. David expressed his confidence in his God: "In my distress I called upon the Lord, yes, I cried to my God; and from His temple He heard my voice, and my cry for help came into His ears" (v. 7).

This song, which is almost identical to Psalm 18, records David's experiences of being hunted, surrounded, trapped, and frustrated by his enemies. These people were far more than personal enemies to David. They were reasons to call down the punishment and deliverance of the Most High God.

The forces of evil were coming at David, but God was his Stronghold, his Deliverer. He spoke of God's mighty deliverance on a cosmic scale: "The earth shook and quaked, the foundations of heaven were trembling and were shaken. . . . He bowed the heavens. . . . He rode on a cherub and flew; and He appeared on the wings of the wind. . . . He sent from on high, He took me; He drew me out of many waters."

David then spoke of his own cleanness before God. Knowing his life as we do, we wonder how he could cry out with such confidence and beauty to God. I think the key lies in the phrase "according to my cleanness before His eyes" (v. 25). David's confidence was not in his own behavior, but rather in the mercy, grace, and forgiveness of God. David was reconciled to God repeatedly by his repentance. He was a man after God's own heart because he repented thoroughly of his sin before the Lord. David did not continue deliberately in sin. Although his volcanic personality caused him to sin on many occasions, he always came to God in true repentance, and God never failed to respond in forgiveness.

David spoke of how God deals with people. He then turned to his own great strength, which seemed to come from God's deliverance of his chosen one, and also from David's purity of heart before God. (See vv. 28-31.)

The song finishes with thanks to God: "Therefore I will give thanks to Thee, O Lord, among the nations, and I will sing praises to Thy name. He is a tower of deliverance to His king, and shows lovingkindness to His anointed, to David and his descendants forever" (vv. 50-51).

Talk about a song of a soul set free! David saw himself as God's anointed, and therefore a person under the protective hand of God. He sensed God's purpose for his life, and experienced the great strength which he had received to accomplish God's will.

This song has a universal appeal in that it is not only David's story, but the experience of any person who has waged an uphill battle against great odds, traveling the hard road of misunderstanding and rejection. If he is living before God with purity of heart, and obeying the commands of God, he can wait with confidence, knowing that God will deliver him.

Prophecy in Verse

In 2 Samuel 23:1-7, we read the last words of David the king. I don't know if these are his last actual words or his last official words. The verses are divided into five sections.

In verse 1, David identified himself as the son of Jesse; as the man who became powerful in war and peace; as the anointed and chosen of God; and as the sweet psalmist. As a poet who recorded the songs of the people and wrote more of his own, he belonged to the people in a way that he never could have without this gift.

In verses 2 and 3, David established the divine inspiration of the words which God gave to him. He said this in four different ways, so that there would be no doubt.

In verses 3 and 4, he told the word which came to him from

God. The prophecy spoke of the man who rules righteously, comparing him to the light of morning at sunrise, a morning without clouds. This seems to point prophetically to the One who will sit on David's throne forever.

Zacharias, in his prophecy after the birth of John the Baptist, called Christ "the Sunrise from on high" (Luke 1:78). Peter called Him the "Morning Star" who would arise in their hearts (2 Peter 1:19). In the letter to the church of Thyatira, Jesus said, "I will give him the Morning Star" (Rev. 2:28). And of Himself, Jesus said, "I am the Root and the Offspring of David, the bright Morning Star" (Rev. 22:16).

David then spoke of his own household and God's everlasting covenant to him. He expressed confidence that God would make the promise grow, and keep His covenant.

For the Hebrew people of the generations following David, the house of David had special significance, for from it would come the Messiah and the future salvation of Israel.

In verses 6 and 7, David looked forward to the final Day of the Lord, in which judgment of evil would take place. His words remind us of verses in Isaiah and Revelation. (See Isa. 19:17 and Rev. 19:15.)

We don't usually think of David as a prophet, and yet to him was given this far-reaching prophecy that would affect all the people of the world.

Mighty Men

Second Samuel 23:8-39 lists the mighty men who were with David in the wilderness, and tells a few of their most famous deeds. This is a very brief recording of these legendary men, of whom many stories must have been told through the years.

The chief three of the men were Josheb-basshebeth or Adino the Eznite, Eleazar the son of Dodo, and Shammah the son of Agee. These three had come to David in the cave of Adullam which was in the valley of Rephaim.

Once during the wilderness days, David had craved water from the well of Bethlehem. But there was a complication to obtaining the water—the Philistines were in Bethlehem. In great loyalty and love, three of David's men broke through the camp of the Philistines. They drew water from the well of Bethlehem and went back to present this gift to David. He was so overwhelmed that he would not drink the water, but poured it out on the ground as an offering to the Lord. He said, "Be it far from me, O Lord, that I should do this. Shall I drink the blood of the men who went in jeopardy of their lives?" (23:17) David was a man of principle and lived accordingly.

Abishai, brother to Joab, was chief of 30 men, and was the most honored of the 30, although his greatness wasn't quite up to that of the three most mighty men. However, he was at David's side, frequently offering to make heads roll if David so desired.

Asahel, Joab's brother who was killed by Abner, was one of the 30. Benaiah we have met before in 2 Samuel 8:18. David made him chief over his guard. Eliam was the son of Ahithophel and father of Bathsheba. Ira the Ithrite is thought to be the priest mentioned in 2 Samuel 20:26.

As the roll call continues, most of the names are not familiar to us. However, the last name, Uriah, strikes a familiar bell, since he was Bathsheba's husband.

Frequently we read in the Bible of people who are simply identified as "a certain man" or "a certain woman." Their names are not recorded, even though they may have done something that changed the course of events in their society. But they are known to God, as we are. We need to remember that God is very much aware of the details of our lives—our hopes, needs and dreams, our work and our pleasures.

In the New Testament there is another roll call, in Hebrews 11, which lists people who were not necessarily mighty in war, but were mighty in their faith. We are all invited to belong to this list. As David's mighty men had faith in him and in his God, so we too are invited to have faith in David's God and to know Him in the same quality of closeness that David experienced.

Numbering the People

Second Samuel 24 tells us that the anger of the Lord incited David to number the people. In 1 Chronicles 21:1, it says, "Then Satan stood up against Israel and moved David to number Israel."

David told Joab, "Go about now through all the tribes of Israel, from Dan to Beersheba, and register the people, that I may know the number of the people" (2 Sam. 24:2).

Joab was aware that this numbering was not pleasing to God and asked David why he wanted to do it: "Now may the Lord your God add to the people a hundred times as many as they are, while the eyes of my lord the king still see; but why does my lord the king delight in this thing?" Joab was right, but the king prevailed "against Joab and against the commanders of the army" (24:3-4).

This is certainly an example of a time when David did not listen to advice. However, when we remember this occurred during the growing rebellion of Absalom, it is easier to understand why David wanted the census.

The census took almost 10 months, and involved Joab and all of the commanders, as they went through the land. The number they came back with was "800,000 valiant men who drew the sword" (v. 9) in Israel, and 500,000 in Judah.

Penitence and Pestilence

After David had received the number, his heart began to be troubled and he said to the Lord, "I have sinned greatly in what I have done. But now, O Lord, please take away the iniquity of Thy servant, for I have acted very foolishly" (24:10).

Though David recognized his sin, the judgment of God for that sin would confront him. The consequences of sin do not just go away. God is love, but He also administers judgment. The Word of the Lord came to Gad, who was the king's seer, presenting to him three options from which David could choose. All three were unpleasant, to say the least—seven years of famine in the land, three months of fleeing from an enemy, or three days of pestilence.

David's response was typical of this man of God. "I am in great distress. Let us now fall into the hand of the Lord for His mercies are great, but do not let me fall into the hand of man" (v. 14). David had great confidence in the mercy of God. He knew that he had sinned and that there were consequences to pay, but he put the choice of those consequences into God's hands.

The Lord sent the pestilence upon Israel for three days and 70,000 men died. "When the angel stretched out his hand toward Jerusalem to destroy it, the Lord relented from the calamity, and said to the angel who destroyed the people, 'It is enough! Now relax your hand!' And the angel of the Lord was by the threshing floor of Araunah the Jebusite" (24:16).

When David saw the angel who was killing the people, he spoke to him, "Behold, it is I who have sinned, and it is I who have done wrong; but these sheep, what have they done? Please let Thy hand be against me and against my father's house" (v. 17). David shouldered the responsibility of his own failure in a very manly way.

The Prophet Gad returned to David, suggesting that he raise an altar to the Lord at the threshing floor of Araunah, and David went to do so. One thing about David was his ability to take instructions and respond immediately. Jesse had raised his young shepherd son well, teaching him obedience in little things. This training was reflected in David's behavior as king of Israel.

An Offering of Value

The story that follows is touching. Araunah recognized David and bowed himself before the king, asking why he had come to the threshing floor. David offered to buy the floor to build his altar so that the plague might be stopped.

Araunah's response was most generous—he offered the use of his threshing floor, and his oxen for a burnt offering. In addition David could use the threshing sledges and the yokes of the oxen for the wood. David's immediate need would be completely met by Araunah.

Do you know anybody like that? I can think of three men who have come into my life who have this attitude of generosity. They convey the feeling that if they have the resources, there isn't anything that they wouldn't do for you. Each of the three has an amazing selflessness. The last time I saw one of them, he greeted me warmly and then said, "Paul, what can I do for you?"

Now you may be thinking that Araunah had a personal interest in the sacrifice being offered. He wanted to get the plague over with, just like everyone else did. But even considering this, he could have felt deep anger at David for being the cause of the plague in the first place.

David responded to Araunah's generous offer by saying, "No, but I will surely buy it from you for a price, for I will not offer burnt offerings to the Lord my God *which cost me nothing*" (v. 24). He purchased the threshing floor and the oxen from Araunah and built an altar to the Lord, offering burnt offerings and peace offerings. And the Lord responded by stopping the pestilence in the land.

David's insistence on paying for what he would offer is an example for us as we realize how hard it is to consistently consider God first in the use of our money, our time, and our talents. We have a tendency to take the easy way out, and give God what is left over. David's statement remains a challenge today: "I will not offer burnt offerings to the Lord my God which cost me nothing."

David's offering was one of flesh and blood, to ask mercy from the Lord for his sin. God made an offering for sin that cost Him everything. He sent His only Son to live and die on earth, to pay the price for our sins. God could not offer what cost Him nothing, or even merely something—it cost Him everything. He heard His Son cry out from the cross—"My God, My God, why hast Thou forsaken Me?"

That is what God wants from us, everything, not as an offering for our sins, but as a rational or "spiritual service of worship," because of what God has done for us. The Apostle Paul urged the Roman Christians by the mercies of God, to present their bodies "a living and holy sacrifice, acceptable to God" (Rom. 12:1).

The purchase of this threshing floor meant a great deal to David, for later he chose this very place as the site of the future temple. But first he had to pay the price or he could not give it to God.

מָגֵן דָּוִד

12
The
Golden Years

1 KINGS 1—2 and 1 CHRONICLES 22—29

King David was old, advanced in age; and they covered him with clothes, but he could not keep warm. So his servants said to him, "Let them seek a young virgin for my lord the king, and let her attend the king and become his nurse; and let her lie in your bosom, that my lord the king may keep warm."

So they searched for a beautiful girl throughout all the territory of Israel, and found Abishag the Shunammite, and brought her to the king.

And the girl was very beautiful; and she became the king's nurse and served him, but the king did not cohabit with her (1 Kings 1:1-4).

Now that is a rather earthy way of letting us know the condition of David. His servants, fully aware of his passion and lifestyle, thought such a solution would be pleasing and helpful to David. I am not sure what they had in mind with the beautiful and young Abishag serving and cherishing the king, but there is no question in that last phrase, "the king knew her not" (KJV). When we came to this section in Homebuilders' Class, I mentioned to my wife Janet about the servants bringing Abishag in to keep David warm, and she said, "Isn't it a shame they didn't have electric blankets!"

We know that David was almost 70 years old at this time. However, from a medical point of view, the chronological age of a person is not as important as his physiological age, and David was an old man physiologically, and close to death.

Who Will Be King?

When a king is near death, there is always the question of succession. David's first son, Amnon, was long dead. The second son, Chileab, either had died or was unfit to reign. The third son, Absalom, was also dead.

This brings us to Adonijah, son of Haggith. He was helping David rule before Solomon was born. (See 2 Sam. 8:18.) When he thought his father would soon die, he decided he was next in line for the throne and would begin to enjoy the favor of the people now. So "he prepared for himself chariots and horsemen with 50 men to run before him" (1 Kings 1:5).

We are given an amazing insight into Adonijah's relationship with David: "And his father had never crossed him at any time by asking, 'Why have you done so?' And he was also a very handsome man" (v. 6).

Again, David had problems with one of his children, and this time it was because he had failed to make clear his desires for succession to the throne. We see problems of this type today, especially in the disposition of the estate after parents die. If there is not a will stating exactly how things should be divided, adult children, with more than adequate money of their own, can get into terrible hassles with brothers and sisters over the inheritance.

Adonijah had convinced his uncle Joab and Abiathar the priest to support him as king. However, the rest of David's men had remained loyal to the king.

To celebrate, Adonijah planned a great feast, for which he killed sheep, oxen, and fatted cattle. He invited all of his brothers, except Solomon, and all the men of Judah to come to the Slippery Stone near En-rogel. However, he did not invite Nathan the prophet, Benaiah who was over David's guard, or the mighty men.

Nathan and Bathsheba

Nathan's sources of information were accurate, and when he realized the full impact of what was happening, he went to Bathsheba to ask if she knew that Adonijah was proclaiming himself king. Since neither she nor David was aware of this, Nathan asked Bathsheba to allow him to advise her in a way that would save her life and the life of Solomon, and insure that Solomon would become king.

He asked her to go in to David and begin to tell him of the events, and that he, Nathan, would follow shortly afterward.

Bathsheba, following Nathan's instruction, entered David's room where Abishag was ministering to him. An American wife would have seen red about this time, and might have forgotten what she came in to say. But with the oriental custom of multiple wives, the Jewish women were apparently not as possessive as our ladies.

Bathsheba bowed before David and he asked her what she wanted. She first reminded him of his promise to her that Solomon would become king, a promise made as a vow by the name of the Lord God.

"And now, behold, Adonijah is king; and now, my lord the king, you do not know it." She told him of the feast and who was invited and then said, "As for you now, my lord the king, the eyes of all Israel are on you, to tell them who shall sit on the throne of my lord the king after him. Otherwise it will come about, as soon as my lord the king sleeps with his fathers, that I and my son Solomon will be considered offenders" (1:18-21).

The Prophet Nathan was then announced, with some ceremony.

He entered the room where David was and prostrated himself before he asked,

> My lord the king, have you said, "Adonijah shall be king after me, and he shall sit on my throne"? For he has gone down today and has sacrificed oxen and fatlings and sheep in abundance, and has invited all the king's sons and the commanders of the army and Abiathar the priest, and behold, they are eating and drinking before him; and they say, "Long live King Adonijah!"

> But me, even me your servant, and Zadok the priest and Benaiah the son of Jehoiada, and your servant Solomon, he has not invited. Has this thing been done by my lord the king, and you have not shown to your servants who should sit on the throne of my lord the king after him? (vv. 24-27)

Bathsheba had left the room when Nathan entered, and now David asked his servants to bring her back. As she stood beside him, he said, "As the Lord lives, who has redeemed my life from all distress, surely as I vowed to you by the Lord the God of Israel, saying, 'Your son Solomon shall be king after me, and he shall sit on my throne in my place'; I will indeed do so this day" (vv. 29-30). Bathsheba prostrated herself before David and said, "May my lord King David live forever" (v. 31).

David was finally realizing just how old and close to death he was. He agreed to take care of the succession that very day. I often see in older people a reluctance to admit how old they are, and a procrastination about putting their affairs in order. I have had many patients with broken hips who refused to go to nursing homes because they didn't want to be around all those old people. The oldest one I recall saying this was 92 years old.

Solomon the King

The only way Solomon was going to be king was for David to designate him through the proper legal procedures of the kingdom. Just deciding that Solomon would follow him would not make him king. David promptly made arrangements for his son to be legally crowned king. He called for Zadok the priest, for Nathan, and for Benaiah to come into his presence. He told them to have

Solomon ride on the king's mule to Gihon where Zadok and Nathan would anoint him king over Israel. After blowing the trumpet and proclaiming, "Long live King Solomon!" they were to bring him back to sit on David's throne as king.

Benaiah gave the response for the three when he said, "Amen! Thus may the Lord, the God of my lord the king, say. As the Lord has been with my lord the king, so may He be with Solomon, and make his throne greater than the throne of my lord King David!" (vv. 36-37)

Zadok, Nathan, and Benaiah did as David had directed, but they invited a few other people along also: the Cherethites and the Pelethites, because after all, you can't crown a king and cheer him properly with only three participants. The reason they could so easily persuade these two groups of foreigners to come was that Benaiah was their chief. (See 2 Sam. 8:18.)

Crowds attract crowds, and after Solomon was anointed, many people followed after him, playing on flutes and rejoicing so loudly that "the earth shook at their noise." Adonijah and his guests at the feast heard the noise just as they were finishing their meal. Joab asked, "Why is the city making such an uproar?" (See 1 Kings 1:40-41.) Just then Jonathan, Abiathar's son, came in to tell them that Solomon was the new king. Jonathan had the full story: including the fact that Solomon had already sat on David's throne.

Adonijah's guests were so terrified at this news that they fled to their homes. They knew that no matter how much celebrating they did, David had followed the legal and accepted route, and Solomon was now their king.

Adonijah at the Altar

Adonijah was so afraid that he ran to the tent of the Lord where he took hold of the horns of the altar. The word was conveyed to Solomon that Adonijah wanted assurances, while still holding on to the horns of the altar, that Solomon would not kill him.

The altar, as a place of sacrifice, was ordinarily a place of refuge. The horns of the altar were considered the most holy part and were associated with the prayers of the saints.

Solomon's answer was, "If he will be a worthy man, not one of his hairs will fall to the ground; but if wickedness is found in him, he will die" (1:52). Then Solomon sent messengers who brought Adonijah down from the altar. Solomon told his brother to go home.

Solomon, the son of David and Bathsheba, was now on the throne of Israel. Although David and Bathsheba, along with the entire nation, had paid dearly for their sin, God in His grace and mercy permitted and even chose their son to be the third king of Israel. Though we make tragic errors and sin greatly, if we are truly penitent, our lives can be reestablished, and God's purposes for our lives accomplished.

Preparation for Building the Temple

From the time that Solomon was born, about 20 years before David's death, David had been collecting material for the temple which Solomon would build. Part of this material came from the people, but most of it came from plundering enemy cities after wars.

As a site for the temple, he selected the threshing floor which he had bought from Araunah. During all those years, stonecutters hewed out stones, and ironworkers prepared nails and clamps. David bought vast amounts of cedar and more bronze than could be weighed. Because Solomon was so young during most of this preparation, David wanted to supervise it, and have everything ready for Solomon.

Also, I am sure that it brought joy to his heart to have this important part in building the temple. David amassed 100,000 talents of gold; 1,000,000 talents of silver; bronze and iron which could not be weighed because of its abundance; he also obtained the services of skilled craftsmen. (See 1 Chron. 22:14.)

How could David collect such a quantity unless he had a plan in mind? And he did have a plan, which he later told Solomon had been given to him by the Lord. " 'All this,' said David, 'The Lord made me understand in writing by His hand upon me, all the details of this pattern' " (1 Chron. 28:19).

The story of David's preparation for the temple is told to us in 1 Chronicles 22—29. In chapter 22, we read of an earlier conversation with Solomon, in which David explained to him his task for the future. We can imagine that father and son spent much time together gathering materials and making plans for the crafting and placing of the many valuable articles they were accumulating.

After David crowned his son as king, he found the strength to see to the important details of temple service that would be needed. After ordering a census of the Levites who were over 30 years of age, he appointed 24,000 to oversee the work of the temple, 6,000 as officers and judges, 4,000 as gatekeepers, and 4,000 as musicians. The ordering of the temple service was given in detail, and is recorded in 1 Chronicles 23—26.

Silver Threads Among the Gold

As we approach our golden years, it is important to make preparations to pass along our responsibilities to someone else. It is one thing to be forcibly retired from our employment, but it is quite another to make provisions in other areas of life. We all have duties aside from our work that are important. If we are in God's family and serving Him, we have spiritual responsibilities and legacies to pass along to others. It grieves me to see men who are obviously growing old and who are unwilling to groom younger people to continue their work. I have seen this happen among pastors, principals of Christian schools, presidents of Christian colleges, as well as among doctors.

When a doctor reaches 70 years of age, his surgical privileges are reviewed yearly by the hospital executive medical staff. In many hospitals, when he reaches 75, he will no longer be permitted to do surgery. Often the last person to realize that he has lost his surgical judgment and skill is the surgeon himself!

While David's physical powers had declined, he still had a memory for details that needed to be cared for before he died. Medically speaking, we realize that as people get older, they are very capable of remembering many details—often from years past. Their problem is that they have difficulty remembering what they had for breakfast, or if they had breakfast at all!

An Assembly of Leaders

In 1 Chronicles 28, there is a description of a meeting which David called. He invited "all the officials of Israel, the princes of the tribes, and the commanders of the divisions that served the king, and the commanders of thousands, and the commanders of hundreds, and the overseers of all the property and livestock belonging to the king and his sons, with the officials and the mighty men, even all the valiant men" (v. 1).

He wanted these leaders to know exactly what was going to happen. Chapter 28 describes a very dramatic public meeting, in which David spoke first to the leaders and then to Solomon, in front of the assembly. He related how God had denied him his desire to build the temple, but had given him Solomon to fulfill the dream and complete the task.

Then he admonished the leaders to seek after the commandments of God so that they might possess the land and bequeath it to their sons after them.

David then turned to Solomon and said, "As for you, my son Solomon, know the God of your father, and serve Him with a whole heart and a willing mind; for the Lord searches all hearts, and understands every intent of the thoughts. If you seek Him, He will let you find Him; but if you forsake Him, He will reject you forever" (v. 9).

David turned their attention to the temple as he gave Solomon the plans for the temple, its buildings, storehouses, and all the rooms inside and out. He also gave him the orders of service for the Levites and specified the amount of gold that should be in the utensils of service and in the ornamental objects.

Then David said to his son Solomon, "Be strong and courageous, and act; do not fear nor be dismayed, for the Lord God, my God, is with you. He will not fail you nor forsake you until all the work for the service of the house of the Lord is finished.

"Now behold, there are the divisions of the priests and the Levites for all the service of the house of God, and every willing man of any skill will be with you in all the work for all kinds of service. The officials also and all the people will be entirely at your command" (1 Chron. 28:20-21).

Picture a 20-year-old king, newly crowned, with his aged father charging him in the presence of the very people who could "make him" or "break him" as he assumed his rule. The effect is dramatic—David was binding the leaders to his son, emphasizing their dependence on each other.

As parents, will you and I give such clear instructions to our children? Are we so spiritually oriented that we will make abundantly clear to our grown children that they have a legacy from us and a responsibility to the Lord and to others?

We have all seen the tragic instances of young persons being thrust into responsibilities for which they have little qualification beyond their good looks and charm, and in which they are left to sink or swim almost totally on their own. No mentors are helping, supporting, guiding, or befriending. No provision has been made for orderly instruction or assumption of authority. When a young person fails, and many do, an older observer may stand back and say, "What could you expect?"

David was not about to let this happen to Solomon. He turned to the assembly of leaders to say, "My son Solomon, whom alone God has chosen, is still young and inexperienced and the work is great; for the temple is not for man, but for the Lord God" (29:1).

Frequently, churches build sanctuaries for particular ministers. Although a pastor may be very gifted, he and the congregation must be careful to realize that they are building a house for God. Any man may suffer illness, disability, premature death, or be called to another place. The building and the people remain, and their loyalty must be established to the work of God, rather than to a pastor. "For the temple is not for man, but for the Lord God."

David then reminded the leaders of his own contributions to the house of God, and offered them the opportunity to give also. They brought large amounts of material to be used, and "rejoiced because they had offered so willingly, for they made their offering to the Lord with a whole heart, and King David also rejoiced greatly" (29:9). With all that David had gathered for 20 years, along with the contributions of the people, they certainly were not going to be paying for the temple for the next 20 years.

Any modern building program which is based on this type of commitment and financial solvency will succeed. Modern churches would do well to learn this lesson. David had thoroughly prepared and provided for all aspects of construction. His capital funds drive was an overwhelming success. Yet David's attitude remained consistent, as a man called of God.

Final Prayers

After the people had brought their gifts, David praised the Lord in one of the most remarkable prayers in Scripture.

Thine, O Lord, is the greatness and the power and the glory and the victory and the majesty, indeed everything that is in the heavens and the earth; Thine is the dominion, O Lord and Thou dost exalt Thyself as head over all.

Both riches and honor come from Thee, and Thou dost rule over all, and in Thy hand is power and might; and it lies in Thy hand to make great, and to strengthen everyone. . . . But who am I and who are my people that we should be able to offer as generously as this? For all things come from Thee, and from Thy hand we have given Thee. For we are sojourners before Thee, and tenants, as all our fathers were. . . .

O Lord our God, all this abundance that we have provided to build Thee a house for Thy holy name, it is from Thy hand, and all is Thine (29:11-16).

Then David urged the leaders to bless the Lord, and they all bowed and paid homage to the Lord and to the king. The next day was a feast day, as they offered 1,000 each of bulls, rams, and lambs, and then ate and drank before the Lord with gladness.

Solomon was proclaimed king a second time, and he sat on the throne of his father; but here it is called "the throne of the Lord."

David's Legacy to Solomon

Realizing that he was going to die soon, David called Solomon to him and charged him with these words:

I am going the way of all the earth. Be strong, therefore, and show yourself a man. And keep the charge of the Lord your God, to walk in His ways, to keep His statutes, His commandments, His ordinances, and His testimonies, according to what is written in the Law of Moses, that you may succeed in all that you do and wherever you turn, so that the Lord may carry out His promise which He spoke concerning me, saying, "If your sons are careful of their way, to walk before Me in truth with all their heart and with all their soul, you shall not lack a man on the throne of Israel" (1 Kings 2:2-4).

The best legacy a man can leave his son is what David left to Solomon in his charge to follow the Word of God. I wonder how many Christian fathers really challenge their sons in this way, or even consider such a challenge.

If your children are to succeed, they must be admonished to keep the commandments of God. There is no better foundation upon which to stand.

As your children get older, you need to consistently challenge them about service for God. If you do this, you can confidently tell them, "You will succeed in your life, if you seek the Lord and follow His Word." (See 1 Chron. 22:11-19.)

Success by God's standard does not necessarily mean money or power. Your children may be poor in this world's goods and relatively unknown. But they can still succeed in a work that gives deep satisfaction if they are involved in a life with eternal values.

As parents we have to be careful that we don't mix our priorities and equate success with being a millionaire or a prominent business or professional person. We need to think of success as God defines it.

David's Warning to Solomon

The second part of David's charge to Solomon was concerned with people whom he felt would cause Solomon trouble. Because of Joab's murder of Abner and Amasa, and because of the way he waged war in bloody fashion, David didn't trust Joab to be of help to Solomon. Shimei, who had cursed David, was under a vow that he would not be punished by David. But Solomon would be free to do whatever he thought best. David also asked that the new king show kindness to the sons of Barzillai who had been so good to David when he was fleeing from Absalom. David then died, and Solomon was established as king.

These warnings which David gave to his son remind me of the warnings which are necessary to give to our children today. If we know their friends, we can be more aware of specific needs, or potential problems. A common problem today is shoplifting. If one of your children happens to be along with someone who is caught shoplifting, your child is going to be in trouble too. He needs to know this ahead of time.

Another difficult situation arises from the way some teens drive their cars. When observing these reckless drivers, I have told my kids, "If I *ever* see you driving like that! . . . Furthermore, if you are in a car where the driver is driving carelessly, I want you to get out and phone me immediately. I will come to get you, any time and any place. Don't ride in a car being driven recklessly."

The Death of David

The writers of 1 Kings and 1 Chronicles described David's death in these words:

Then David slept with his fathers and was buried in the city of David. And the days that David reigned over Israel were 40 years: 7 years he reigned in Hebron, and 33 years he reigned in Jerusalem (1 Kings 2:10-11).

Then he died in a ripe old age, full of days, riches, and honor; and his son Solomon reigned in his place. Now the acts of King David, from first to last, are written in the chronicles of Samuel the seer, in the chronicles of Nathan the prophet, and in the chronicles of Gad the seer, with all his reign, his power, and the circumstances which came on him, on Israel, and on all the kingdoms of the lands (1 Chron. 29:28-30).

David's life on this earth was over, and yet there were a few matters that had to be taken care of, before Solomon's kingship could be established.

Adonijah's Request

Adonijah paid a visit to Bathsheba to request a favor. He wanted her to ask Solomon if he could have Abishag the Shunammite as his wife. (See 1 Kings 2:13-17.) Bathsheba agreed to convey the request.

When she went in to talk with Solomon, he rose to meet her, bowed before her, and then sat down on his throne, with Bathsheba on a special throne to his right. Even though he was now king, his mother was still his mother, and he obviously respected and loved her.

I like this description of the king and his mother. When children are in their early teens (sometimes described as a stage of temporary insanity), they have a tendency to talk to their mothers disrespectfully. It is best to deal with the problem promptly. It is the father's responsibility to see that the conversation demonstrates proper respect for their mother, *at all times. "She is your mother!"* This is the foundation of a relationship such as King Solomon had with his mother.

When Solomon heard what Adonijah wanted, he said to his mother, "You might as well ask for the kingdom for Adonijah, and for Joab and Abiathar too. Adonijah has just decreed his own death." And Solomon sent Benaiah to kill Adonijah (2:22-25).

Adonijah knew his request was outrageous. Abishag was considered a concubine to David, even though there were not intimate relations between them. It was customary for a new king to inherit the harem of a deceased king. Because Bathsheba probably knew all this too, I am not sure she conveyed Adonijah's request in good faith. She may have known what would happen.

Abiathar

This was the priest who had come to David after his father Ahimelech and 85 priests had been killed by Doeg. Because he was with David during the wilderness wanderings, we know that he was not a young man.

Solomon's word to him was, "Go to Anathoth to your own field, for you deserve to die; but I will not put you to death at this

time, because you carried the Ark of the Lord God before my
father David, and because you were afflicted in everything with
which my father was afflicted" (2:26).

Joab
When Joab heard of Adonijah's death, he ran to the tent of the
Lord and took hold of the horns of the altar. Once again Solomon
called on Benaiah, telling him to kill Joab this time. Benaiah
entered the tent and ordered Joab out, but he refused to leave,
saying, "No, for I will die here."

Benaiah returned to Solomon with Joab's response. He didn't
want to kill Joab in front of the altar. To understand this, and Solomon's subsequent order to kill him right there, we need to look
back to Exodus 21:14: "If, however, a man acts presumptuously
toward his neighbor, so as to kill him craftily, you are to take him
even from My altar, that he may die."

What Solomon said to Benaiah now was this: "Do as he has
spoken and fall upon him and bury him, that you may remove
from me and from my father's house the blood which Joab shed
without cause" (1 Kings 2:31).

After Benaiah carried out the king's order, he was appointed
as commander in Joab's place, and Zadok was named as priest
in place of Abiathar.

Shimei
This man was dealt with differently than the others, in that he
was allowed to live, as long as he did not cross the brook Kidron
to leave the area. He agreed to this and lived in Jerusalem. However, after three years, two of his servants ran away to Gath. When
he heard where they were, he went in pursuit of them. While this
seems a natural reaction for a man, it was not excusable as far
as Solomon was concerned. Shimei lost his life for not keeping
his part of the agreement.

The Impact of a Good Life
A man like David makes a remarkable impression upon his own
time. But what about a generation later? A millennium later?

I think it is safe to say that no other Old Testament figure has had a greater impact upon the history, hopes, and dreams of the Jewish nation. To succeeding generations, David was irrevocably linked to their hope of a Messiah, and of a kingdom of peace and abundance. Even today David is highly regarded by the Israelis. They see him as a model for military courage and as a champion of political independence.

Phrases including David's name became part of the lore of Israel—phrases such as, "a shoot from the stem of Jesse; a judge in the tent of David; key of the house of David; the mercies of David; My covenant with David; the Son of David; the throne of His father David."

When the people of Jesus' time called Him "Son of David," they were really saying *Messiah*. In the days of the early church, when the Apostles wanted to present the legitimacy of Christ's claim to be God, they quoted David, or referred to the prophecies which used his name.

One such time was on the Day of Pentecost. Peter began his sermon (Acts 2:14-36) with a prophecy from the Book of Joel, and then spoke of Jesus. To prove what he was saying, Peter referred to David, the patriarch and prophet, who "looked ahead and spoke of the resurrection of the Christ."

Peter then moved on to the glorification of Christ and again quoted David to prove his point; "The Lord said to my Lord, 'Sit at My right hand, until I make Thine enemies a footstool for Thy feet.'"

He ended his sermon with these words: "Therefore, let all the house of Israel know for certain that God has made Him both Lord and Christ—this Jesus whom you crucified."

When the people heard this, they were "pierced to the heart, and said to Peter and the rest of the Apostles, 'Brethren, what shall we do?'"

They had heard the Gospel according to David.

FRIENDS, RELATIVES, AND ENEMIES OF DAVID

Jesse—David's father

Jesse's children—Eliab, Abinadab, Shimea, Nethanel, Raddai, Ozem, Zeruiah, Abigail, David

David's nephews—Jonadab, friend to Amnon; Abishai, commander of the 30 men; Joab, commander of David's army; Asahel

David's wives and their children

Michal

Ahinoam—Amnon

Abigail—Daniel or Chileab

Maacah—Absalom and Tamar

Haggith—Adonijah

Abital—Shephatiah

Eglah—Ithream

Bathsheba—Shammua, Shobab, Nathan, Jedidiah or Solomon

Other wives' sons—Ibhar, Elishua, Eliphelet, Nogah, Nepheg, Japhia, Elishama, Eliada, Eliphelet the second

Saul—first king of Israel

Saul's children—Jonathan, Abinadab, Malchishua, Ishbosheth, Merab, Michal

Abner—Saul's first cousin and general

Mephibosheth—son to Jonathan and crippled

Ziba—servant of Mephibosheth

Rizpah—concubine to Saul and Abner

Prophets—Samuel, Nathan, Gad

Priests—Ahimelech, Abiathar, Zadok, Jonathan, Ahimaaz

Military men—Abner, Saul's general; Joab, David's general; Amasa, nephew to David; Abishai; Ittai the Gittite; Uriah the Hittite; Benaiah, head of David's guard.

Kings—Talmai, king of Geshur, and grandfather of Absalom and Tamar; Hiram, king of Tyre; Achish, king of Gath.

Others—Ahithophel, counselor to David and Absalom; Nabal, husband to Abigail; Doeg the Edomite who killed 85 priests; witch of Endor; Goliath the giant; Palti, second husband to Michal; Araunah, owner of the threshing floor; Hushai, David's friend who falsely counseled Absalom; Abishag, young woman who warmed David in his old age; Barzillai, old man who blessed David.

Spellings of proper names are taken from NASB.

Scriptures for Further Study about David

ISAIAH 4:2; 9:6-7; 11:1; 11:10; 16:5; 22:22; 28:16; 37:35; 53:2; 55:3.
JEREMIAH 2:13; 17:13; 23:5-6; 30:9; 33:15-17; 33:21.
HOSEA 3:5.
AMOS 6:5; 9:11.
EZEKIEL 34:22-24; 37:24-25.
ZECHARIAH 3:8; 6:12; 12:7-10; 13:1; 13:7-8; 14:3-4.
MATTHEW 1:1; 9:27; 12:3; 12:23; 12:42; 21:9; 22:42; 1:6; 22:45; 20:30; 15:22.
MARK 10:47-48.
LUKE 1:27; 1:69; 1:32; 2:4.
JOHN 7:42.
ACTS 2:29, 34; 4:24-25; 7:45-46; 13:22-23; 13:33-36.
ROMANS 4:6-8; 1:3; 15:12.
HEBREWS 4:7; 11:32.
REVELATION 1:18; 5:5; 3:7; 3:3; 22:16.